YOUR ....
CHATTAHOOCHEE
NATIONAL FOREST

A Collection of the Author's Newspaper Columns from December 1978 to June 1980

By Dan Kincaid

Copyright @ 2016 by Dan B. Kincaid

ISBN 13:978-1536842241

ISBN 10:1536842249

Published by: Kade Holley Publishing and Create Space

Editing: Kade Holley

Cover design: Shannon Lough and Kade Holley Publishing

Cover photo courtesy of USDA Forest Service

Printed in the United States of America.

REVIEWS AND READER COMMENTS:

Dan's weekly columns were an excellent means for communicating with the public about the Chattahoochee National Forest in the late 1970's and the early 1980's. He wrote columns about management on the Brasstown Ranger District, human interest stories, and provided general information about the Forest Service. Thank you, my friend, for putting together this important book.
Jack McCormick, Retired District Ranger, U.S. Forest Service

This book is a welcome addition to the historical record of our area. The great outdoors and the Chattahoochee National Forest are integral parts of life in our beautiful north Georgia mountains. These columns feature topics that were timely in 1979-80. Future generations will be glad that these columns have been compiled in this book.
Alan Denmon, President, Union County Historical Society, Blairsville, GA

Those years were wonderful times on the Chattahoochee National Forest. Dan's interest in communicating with the public thru his columns was a great idea. I'm proud to have written a few of these columns myself.
Frances Mason, Retired Forester, Chattahoochee National Forest

DEDICATION

This book is dedicated to the many outstanding employees who have served over the years on the Brasstown Ranger District, Chattahoochee National Forest. Their hard work and professionalism have helped make this national forest one of the finest in the United States.

I would also like to specifically mention Charles Mason, Frances Mason, and Doug Gray, who I worked with from 1978-80. They have remained friends and have kept me informed about current Chattahoochee National Forest events over the past 35+ years.

In addition, Angie Arrant, current Support Services Specialist at the Blairsville office, has been a familiar Forest Service presence since the late 1970s. Beginning as an enrollee in our Young Adult Conservation Corps program, Angie (Henson at the time) has moved thru the ranks, performing all office-related functions at one time or another. I have known her for nearly 40 years and she has been a steadying and positive influence for the Chattahoochee National Forest.

PREFACE AND ACKNOWLEDGEMENTS

The ownership and the staffs at **The North Georgia News** and **The Towns County Herald** were extremely helpful and encouraging to me during the time that I wrote this outdoor column for their newspapers. My columns were either sent or delivered to them (depending upon deadlines) on a weekly basis and with few exceptions were published as submitted.

My supervisor at the Chattahoochee National Forest, District Ranger Jack McCormick, was very supportive of this writing effort, as was his boss, Forest Supervisor, Pat Thomas. They both recognized the value to the U.S. Forest Service of communicating with the public via regular newspaper columns.

Readers in both Towns and Union counties responded favorably to the columns, offering thanks and encouragement, and often suggesting topics for future columns. Reader feedback and support was important in newspaper decisions to continue carrying my columns.

INTRODUCTION

Early in my career with the U.S. Forest Service, I began to realize how important the national forests were to the people living near them. Yes, citizens across the country valued the national forests, but, in particular, the management activities on the national forests affected the local residents the most. That is still the case today.

An effective means of communicating with large numbers of people, especially during the early years of my career in the 1970s and 1980s, was through regular newspaper columns. That allowed an opportunity for contact on a weekly basis and it allowed the opportunity to address numerous topics over the course of a year. Other means of communications, such as community meetings, news releases, one-on-one discussions, and others, were also important; but none offered the sustained contact with large numbers of people that weekly newspaper columns did.

I eventually wrote weekly columns for nearly 12 years – 1978-80 in north Georgia and 1981-90 in southeastern Ohio. The positive feedback I received from readers and community leaders convinced me that the effort was worthwhile and valuable.

Although there have been similar efforts by other Forest Service employees across the country over the years, the numbers have been small, considering all the offices across the United States. I only wish that these kinds of communications activities had received a higher priority by management over the years. If they had, then perhaps some of the problems that the agency encountered with local communities might have been avoided.

As you will notice from reading the columns in this book, my topics ranged widely. I decided early on to include not only the specific Forest Service topics, but also topics on various natural resource and outdoor activities, as well as columns mentioning individuals, groups, and other agencies that would be of interest to readers. I figured that the greater the variety of topics, the greater the number of readers.

The columns in this book are the copies that were submitted to the newspapers. They may have differed just slightly from the final versions that appeared in print. Also, the dates listed on each column were the dates they were submitted, not the dates they actually appeared in the newspapers.

I hope you enjoy reading through these columns. It will give you a historical sense of what was going on nearly 40 years ago – in the Chattahoochee National Forest, the great outdoors, and with natural resource issues of the time.

Prior to beginning this column, I was already very busy. My responsibilities included supervising and managing programs in fire, recreation, special uses, human resource programs, Brasstown Bald Visitor Center, and other various duties. Shortly after starting the column, I was also asked (I think I was "asked," but maybe there's another term for it) to be a member of the Forest Planning Team. Because of these work demands, I was fortunate to have others write some of the columns for me –in fact, about 15 of the 78 or so items in this book were written by others. This was very important because we wanted to maintain the weekly "connection" with the readers.

Three local employees were of tremendous assistance in this effort. Frances Mason wrote five columns for me, Debbie Day wrote four, and Martin Kindred wrote two. Ron Mize, a wildlife biologist stationed at Clarkesville, wrote a column, as did a friend from the Wayne National Forest in Ohio, Ray Schoener. And finally, a Forest Service Engineer, Al Vanderpoel, who I had worked with earlier in my career, wrote two columns for me. Without the assistance of these six individuals, it would have been difficult to keep the newspaper column going in a timely manner. Special thanks to all of them!

I hope you enjoy reading this book as much as I have enjoyed putting it together. Certain items mentioned in the book have changed somewhat over the years, so all of the writings must be kept in the historical perspective of the time. I didn't want to modify the columns for this book. I wanted them to reflect the times in which they were written, 1978-1980 – the times when we were working hard to manage "Your .... Chattahoochee National Forest."

- Dan Kincaid

December 11, 1978 -

Starting today, and then resuming again after the first of the year, I'll be writing a series of weekly columns that are intended to acquaint readers with National Forest activities. More specifically, most of the articles will be centered around activities on the Chattahoochee National Forest. Readers in Union and Towns counties (as well as other subscribers) should find the column interesting and pertinent to their daily lives.

Since North Georgia is so heavily forested, we rely heavily upon the forest environment for much of what we do, whether it be our jobs, our recreation, our drinking water, or any number of other things. The percentage of U.S. Forest Service land in these two counties makes up a substantial amount of the total acreage. Thus, Forest Service activities, policies, and regulations have some degree of impact on almost every resident of Towns and Union counties.

I hope to be able to provide information on our activities so that people will better understand what we're doing, how we're doing it, and most importantly, why we're doing it. There will be information about programs we manage, assistance we offer (or that we might

1

have knowledge of), special activities, career opportunities, and many articles on just plain outdoor and forestry-related items. And for anyone who has a question or concern about the U.S. Forest Service or forestry in general, please don't hesitate to write or stop by our office in Blairsville. The District Ranger or one of his assistants would be glad to talk with you.

Other features in this weekly column will include photographs and short histories of our employees, many of whom you've grown up with and known for years, while others are relative newcomers. Also, many columns will end with an item of special interest or a **Ranger's Notebook** item. These are intended to point out some of the less well known facts about the Forest Service and the profession of forestry.

Well, that's enough for now. I'm looking forward to starting the new column on a regular basis in January and sincerely hope that you will look forward to reading it every week in either the **North Georgia News** or the **Towns County Herald.** Both newspapers have been very supportive and encouraging about this new feature for their weeklies. From everyone on the Brasstown Ranger District, we wish you a Merry Christmas and a very happy New Year.

Ranger's Notebook – The U.S. Forest
Service manages 155 National Forests, 19
National Grasslands, and 17 Land Utilization
Projects totaling about 187 million acres,
located in 44 states, Puerto Rico, and the
Virgin Islands. The Chattahoochee National
Forest contains 744,545 acres across north
Georgia managed out of local offices in
LaFayette, Chatsworth, Blue Ridge, Dahlonega,
Clarkesville, Clayton, and Blairsville. (There are
93,884 National Forest acres in Union County
and 57,182 National Forest acres in Towns
County).

January 5, 1979 –

In this first official column I want to
explain the organization and responsibilities of
the U.S. Forest Service, so that readers will
have a better understanding of our agency.
Many times we're confused with other federal
agencies, such as the National Park Service
(NPS), the Bureau of Land Management
(BLM), or the Soil Conservation Service (SCS).
Other times we're mistaken for state agencies
such as the Georgia Forestry Commission or
the state Department of Natural Resources. In
fact, although we cooperate with all of these

fine agencies in certain land management activities, the Forest Service is an entirely separate organization with different responsibilities.

The Forest Service is part of the U.S. Department of Agriculture, as is the SCS, while the NPS and BLM are part of the U.S. Department of Interior. The Secretary of Agriculture has assigned to the Forest Service the major responsibility of providing leadership in the management, protection, and utilization of the natural resources on all of the national forests and related range lands. These lands cover one-third of this country's surface. The Secretary's delegation of duties also extends the basic activities of National Forest management, as authorized in the Organic Administration Act of 1897, to include responsibilities in State & Private Forestry and Research.

The **National Forest System** is responsible for the management, protection, and development of 187 million acres of national forests and national grasslands. The National Forest System is divided into 10 Regions. (There is no Region 7. Several years ago it was combined partly with Region 8 and partly with Region 9). The Chattahoochee National Forest is in Region 8, the Southern

Region. This Region includes national forests in Georgia, South Carolina, North Carolina, Virginia, Kentucky, Tennessee, Arkansas, Oklahoma, Texas, Louisiana, Mississippi, Alabama, and Florida. The Regional Headquarters is located in Atlanta.

Each Region is divided into several national forests, which have a Supervisor's Office and several Ranger District offices. The Chattahoochee National Forest Supervisor's Office is located in Gainesville and there are Ranger District offices in Blairsville, Clayton, Clarkesville, Dahlonega, Blue Ridge, Chatsworth, and LaFayette.

The Oconee National Forest, located just north of Macon, Georgia, is a separate national forest, but since it is relatively small, it is attached administratively to the Chattahoochee National Forest. That is why you will often see the forests jointly referred to as the Chattahoochee-Oconee National Forest.

National Forests are managed for the continued yields of water, forage, wildlife, wood, and recreation. There are other uses and activities on national forest lands, including fire management, minerals/mining, wilderness, and transportation system management (roads and trails). We also work with environmental education programs; land use planning studies; and work programs for both youths and senior citizens.

The **State & Private Forestry** (S&PF) section of the Forest Service cooperates with state forestry agencies, private landowners, wood industries, universities, and other public agencies and non-profit organizations to help improve management of all of the nation's forest lands. S&PF encourages more scientific management of all forest lands and better utilization of wood resources through both technical and financial assistance.

The **Forest Service Research** branch is the world's largest forestry research organization. Much of the research is conducted in the areas of forest management and wood utilization, but studies are also done in recreation, fire, economics, wildlife management, watershed protection, social sciences, insect & disease control, and several other areas. The ultimate goal of research is to protect and improve the nation's natural resources, while gaining the maximum conservation, economic, and social benefits from their use.

Ranger's Notebook – The National Forests were first authorized by the Creative Act of 1891. President Benjamin Harrison created an area of 1.2 million acres in Wyoming. The Chattahoochee National Forest was formally established 45 years later on July 9, 1936.

January 10, 1979 –

Last week two school children from Union County Elementary stopped by the office. They wanted to know if we had any information about the state tree of Georgia and some of the other southeastern states. We did have the information and it was very interesting sharing this information with the kids.

The state tree of Georgia is the Live Oak, sometimes referred to as Sand Oak. The tree may be unfamiliar to people in north Georgia, since it occurs primarily in the Atlantic and Gulf Coastal Plains from Virginia all the way to Texas. In Georgia the Live Oak is found mostly in the southern third of the state. It is plentiful in the Savannah and Brunswick areas and can be found westward near Waycross, Valdosta, Albany, and Bainbridge. The Live Oak was made the official state tree by the legislature in 1937.

Like all the other oaks, the Live Oak produces acorns, but the leaves of the tree don't look anything at all like typical oak leaves. Live Oak leaves are 2 to 5 inches long, ½ to 2 inches wide, and are dark glossy green on the top. They actually resemble the leaves of our Mountain Laurel or "Ivy."

Live Oak is usually a medium-sized tree 40 to 50 feet high and up to 3 or 4 feet in diameter. The trunk normally divides into wide spreading branches and forms a very wide crown, which makes for a good shade tree. The tree is extremely resistant to salt water spray from the ocean and is often found growing on dunes or dry sand barrens. In these cases Live Oaks are dwarf trees, often only a few feet tall.

The Live Oak is extremely difficult to kill. When someone cuts or girdles the tree, many sprouts spring up from the root collar and surface roots. When these sprouts are cut, many more appear.

The acorns on some of the trees are sweeter and more edible than others. The Indians made an oil from the acorns, something like olive oil.

Though the Live Oak isn't found in Union or Towns County, it is our state tree and that makes it very interesting indeed.

Three of our neighbor states have state trees that are perhaps more familiar to us than the Live Oak. Tennessee's state tree is the

Yellow Poplar or Tulip Poplar, so named because of the tulip-like flowers that it bears in the late Spring. It grows throughout the eastern United States, particularly in moist, mountain coves like those we have in our area.

North Carolina lists its state tree as the Pine and Alabama lists its state tree as the Southern Pine. These actually refer to several trees, including Shortleaf Pine, Longleaf Pine, Loblolly Pine, Slash Pine, Virginia Pine, and in the case of North Carolina, the White Pine. These are all found in Georgia, some of them in our local counties.

South Carolina and Florida both have the same state tree, the Palmetto. The young buds of the tree are edible and, when cooked, taste similar to cabbage – thus the name, Cabbage Palmetto. This tree can be found along the Georgia coast and looks like something out of a tropical jungle.

Ranger's Notebook – The wood of Live Oak is very strong and one of the heaviest of native woods. In the past it was used for building frigates and other Navy ships. The U.S. Navy still owns Live Oak forests, which they bought during the times of "wooden ships and iron men."

"Does it ever snow up here?"

"Are there any elephants in the woods around here?"

"Is it difficult to breathe here because of a lack of oxygen?"

No, these questions aren't about a high mountain peak in Africa or South America. They're questions that visitors to Brasstown Bald Visitor Center asked this past summer. Our Forestry Technicians and Information Specialists at Brasstown Bald are asked questions ranging from those above to "Why do leaves change color?" and "How far is it from here to Phoenix, Arizona?" In short, visitors expect our personnel to be able to answer almost any questions, especially those about natural resources.

The question about snow was asked by a man from the New England states who was surprised that it snowed as far south as Georgia. A man from the country of Zambia wanted to know about the elephants. And a woman from the non-mountainous state of Mississippi was concerned about the lack of oxygen at Brasstown Bald.

Most of the difficult or unusual questions that we get asked are answered by our two permanent employees who normally work at the Visitor Center – Mary Young and Jessie King. During the busy summer months we also hire three to five seasonal employees. Last summer Angie Burns, Lydia Jackson, Dee Rouse, and Gwen Dyer worked for us on Brasstown Bald.

In order to prepare for each Spring's opening at the Visitor Center, one of Mary's winter-time jobs is sorting out and compiling information that will be used in answering visitors' questions. We have a wealth of information about a variety of subjects that we keep on hand for this purpose. While Mary can't hope to memorize all the facts, she tries to familiarize herself with as much as possible. She uses a lot of the material to help train our new summer employees when they come on board in the summer.

Last week Mary summarized our use figures for 1978 and here's what she came up with:

1) We had 65,115 visitors to Brasstown Bald VIS Center last year. Peak months were October (Fall color season) with 24,551 and July with 10,473. Lowest visitor months were December with 81 (we were only

open three days that month) and March with 745.

2) 28,307 visitors signed our guest register, which was 43 percent of the total number of visitors. Our personnel keep total visitor numbers by using the hand-held tally counters.

3) We had visitors from 49 states and the District of Columbia. The missing state? North Dakota. We had eight visitors from Alaska, 17 from Hawaii, 13 from Maine, and 37 from the state of Washington. Wyoming and Vermont had only one visitor each, while Nebraska had two.

4) Approximately 70 percent of our visitors were from Georgia and 13 percent were from Florida. Other states with significant numbers were North Carolina, Tennessee, Alabama, Ohio, South Carolina, Mississippi, Texas, and Louisiana.

5) We had visitors from 40 foreign countries, representing every continent except Antarctica. I

wonder why? We had 72 visitors from England, 53 from Germany, 47 from Canada, and 15 each from Holland and Australia.

6) Among the other countries represented were Taiwan, Zambia, Finland, India, Iraq, Haiti, Israel, Iran, Cuba, Poland, Korea, Turkey, Panama, Japan, Argentina, and France.

Union and Towns counties are hosts, literally, to visitors from all over this country and the world!

Ranger's Notebook – The Southern Region of the U.S. Forest Service operates four major Visitor Centers – Brasstown Bald in Georgia; the Cradle of Forestry in North Carolina; Blanchard Caverns in Arkansas; and Kerr Arboretum in Arkansas. Two smaller visitor facilities are Massanutten Mountain in Virginia and Juniper Springs in Florida.

January 24, 1979 –

Rain, snow, ice, sleet, more rain, and more snow. What terrible weather! These conditions bring a screeching halt to many outdoor activities. And understandably so. But here at the Forest Service this is normally one of our busiest and most active times.

True, recreation use is not heavy now. And certainly there's no danger from forest fires. But in addition to preparing reports, doing paperwork, and making plans for next Spring and Summer, we are currently very busy with our timber program.

For the past couple of months our crews have been doing the following:

1) **White pine release** – This involves cutting down low quality, competing hardwood trees so that the smaller white pines will be exposed to sunlight and have a better chance to grow.

2) **Site preparation** – This involves cutting down old and inferior hardwoods in recent clearcut areas, so that new hardwood seedlings and sprouts can regenerate and grow without the competition.

3) **Timber marking** – This consists of estimating volume and marking trees to be cut in upcoming timber sales.

4) **Pruning** – Cutting off the limbs of white pine trees up to about 16 feet, which increases their future value when sold as sawtimber.

5) **Tree planting** – This job is just beginning and is one of the most important things we do. We'll be planting about 475 acres of pine seedlings, which will take until about mid-April to complete.

6) **Boundary line surveying and marking** – This is an ongoing job that is easiest done in the Winter when all the trees and shrubs have shed their leaves. Much of this work is done in support of our timber sales program.

Yes, through rain, ice, sleet, snow, and just plain old cold weather, the timber job goes on. Doug Gray heads up our timber program and these guys do most of the field work: Don Davenport, J.B. King, Jim Burns, Grady Groves, Charles Hughes, Ronnie Kelley, Crett Dyer, David Burnette, Milton Bradley, Hoyt Browning, Zane Rogers, Danny Owenby, Sheldon Henderson, Charles Mason, L.A. Rich, Ervin Martin, and our YACC crew.

Debbie Day is District Coordinator for what we call our Manpower Programs, which includes the Young Adult Conservation Corps (YACC). The YACC program was enacted by Congress in 1977 to provide manpower to accomplish needed conservation work on public lands and to help curb unemployment for youths between the ages of 16 and 23. Debbie manages the overall program, including hiring, record keeping, and accomplishment reporting; and the day to day work leader is Joe Burnette. Last week eight local young people completed their year in our Brasstown Ranger District YACC program.

At our monthly District Safety Meeting, Burnette and District Ranger Jack McCormick presented certificates to Randy Shope, Vick Payne, Jerry Gilreath, Robert O'Keefe, Bryan Souther, Tony Henderson, Joel Huggins, and David Collins.

Day provided re-cap recognition and listed the projects accomplished by the YACC crew over the past year. This included: wildlife habitat improvement; recreation maintenance and construction; soil and water conservation projects; timber stand improvement; surveying assistance; and road and culvert maintenance.

The Forest Service is very fortunate to have Burnette and the YACC crew available to help conserve and improve natural resources on the Brasstown Ranger District of the Chattahoochee National Forest.

Ranger's Notebook – Our current or new YACC enrollees are Tim Burns, Pat Hacker, Mike Mashburn, Stanley Stepp, Angie Henson, Sonja Adams, Jerry Collins, Darrell Arrowood, Mickey McConnell, Randy McClure, Mary Nichols, Susan White, and Debra McCollum.

February 1, 1979 –

We get a lot of questions here at the office concerning the profession of Forestry and other related fields. Here are three of the most frequently asked questions:

"What does a Forester do?"
Commonly held notions are that Foresters either: 1) Sit in fire towers all day long looking for wildfires; or 2) Spend all day cutting down trees with a chainsaw, like lumberjacks do. Foresters certainly get involved with these activities, but there are many more things with which they get involved.

A Forester is trained to perform a wide variety of jobs which relate to the management and protection of natural resources. This includes wildlife management, insect & disease control, recreation management, fire fighting, land line surveying, timber inventory, water and soil protection, landscape and scenic considerations, conservation education activities, and many other areas as well. The Forester also consults with technical specialists in these fields and then makes wise decisions regarding the proper use of forest land. In practice, the Forester can truly be called a land manager.

"What type of training or experience is required for a forestry job?"

A love of the outdoors is the most basic requirement for working in forestry. But don't think that it will be all hunting, hiking, camping, and fishing. In fact, you'll find that you don't have as much time for those activities as you'd like, because you're too busy working to make sure others can enjoy them.

Educational requirements for Foresters vary slightly and a college degree is required. There is a strong emphasis on science and mathematics during your four years in college.

Nearby schools that offer Bachelors Degrees in Forestry are the University of Georgia, Clemson, Auburn, North Carolina State, and the University of Tennessee.

Forestry Technicians assist Foresters in most management activities. Requirements of a technician job are either: graduating from a two-year Technical School; or having experience and a strong background in outdoor, forestry-related work.

"Are there many job opportunities in the field of Forestry?"

Job opportunities are currently increasing, but so is the competition for them. However, don't let that stop you. If your desire is strong enough, you'll land a job. In addition to the federal government, there are opportunities with state, county, and city governments; private industry; non-profit groups; and consulting or contractual positions.

It's difficult to cover everything in a short column; so, if you have other questions, please stop by our Blairsville office for additional information.

Ranger's Notebook – Bernhard E. Fernow was the first professional Forester in the

United States. He received his education in Germany. He taught the first forestry class in this country at Massachusetts Agricultural College in 1894. The Fernow Experimental Forest, a research area managed by the U.S. Forest Service in West Virginia, was named after him.

February 8, 1979 –

Winter hunting, camping, and hiking are enjoyable activities for many people. They can also be very dangerous, or even fatal, if necessary preparations are not made or proper precautions are not taken. In the summertime minor errors in judgment usually result in only slight inconveniences. However, in the wintertime these same mistakes can accumulate and multiply rapidly, with sometimes tragic results. The following thoughts should be useful to the winter outdoorsman:

1) Travel with a group, or at least with a partner. Then, in case of sickness or injury, someone can go for help.

2) Lay out a reasonable travel route. Generally speaking, most people think they can walk much further than they

actually can. With winter days being very short and snow accumulation slowing your rate of speed, do not over-estimate the distance that you plan to travel. If you're camping, be sure to set up camp early and not get caught by darkness.

3) Know your route well. Be aware of possible hazards. In this part of the country it is best to stay off of lakes or ponds, even if the ice appears to be thick enough to walk on. A plunge in icy water, away from help, can be fatal.

4) Be prepared for the worst! Besides the cold temperatures, the winds are often very strong, particularly on mountains or ridge tops. Extreme wind chill factors can worsen the consequences of any problems you might encounter. At 10 degrees (F) above zero a 25 mile per hour wind causes the chill factor to be 30 degrees below zero! In this instance, exposed flesh can freeze within a very few minutes.

5) Be sure to let someone know where you're going and when you plan to return. If you're not back on time,

rescuers will have an idea where to begin their search.

6) Make sure your vehicle is in good winter driving condition. When you get ready to come home, a car that won't start can spoil your whole trip.

7) Drink plenty of liquids. Dehydration is more common in extreme cold. An adult, at rest, requires about two quarts of water daily. Up to four quarts are required for strenuous activity. There is a 25 percent loss of stamina when an adult loses $1^1/_2$ quarts of water. Avoid dehydration - simply drink as often as you feel thirsty.

8) If you're cold, eat something, drink warm liquids, and put on a cap. Most of the body's heat loss occurs thru the head.

9) Stay dry! When clothes get wet, they lose up to 90 percent of their insulating value. Wool is the exception. It retains a lot of its insulating value even when wet. So, if you're going to be out when it's both wet and cold, wool is your best bet. A

waterproof windbreaker is also very useful in helping to stay warm and dry.

Winter days can be very beautiful. To make sure you have an enjoyable outing: 1) Be prepared; 2) Take necessary precautions; and, 3) Respect nature's rules.

Ranger's Notebook - Hypothermia is the number one killer of outdoor recreationists. It is a subnormal body temperature which, if not reversed, leads to mental and physical collapse. It is caused by exposure to cold, wet, and wind, thus causing body heat loss. A word of warning -- most cases of hypothermia occur in air temperatures between 30 and 50 degrees (F) above zero and during rainy weather; so, you can have problems not only in the Winter, but also in the Spring and Fall.

February 15, 1979 –

This week's article was written by Martin Kindred, a Forester on our District. Martin came to Blairsville in May of 1978 from the Shawnee National Forest in southern Illinois. The majority of his work here involves forest inventory (which he describes below) and wildlife management. Martin grew up in southern Indiana and attended Forestry School at Southern Illinois University. He and his wife, Pat, live on the Murphy Highway.

Forest Inventory - Why and How It's Done

Have you ever wondered how the Forest Service determines where it is going to cut its timber, or what type of cutting method it will use? The procedure we use is called a silvicultural examination. This is a systematic, random-sampling by a professional forester of our management units or compartments. This examination gives us our basic information necessary to manage the forest.

The Brasstown Ranger District contains 112 compartments. The average size for a compartment is about 1,000 acres. Every year we examine about 11 compartments so that by the end of a 10-year period we have examined all of our compartments, and then the process is repeated again and again every 10 years. The continued re-entry and examination of compartments is necessary because the forest is dynamic - always changing. Natural aging, insect and disease attacks, fires, and severe storms are continuously affecting the growth and development of the forest. Without current and accurate data, our management direction can be only a guess.

The professional forester begins an examination by dividing the compartment into stands of similar timber types with the aid of aerial photographs. He then plans out routes of travel, so that he can go to the field and actually walk through all of the "stands" he has identified in the office. (A stand is a forestry term referring to a grouping of similar size, species, and age of trees.) As he is walking through the forest, he stops at pre-determined intervals and gathers data about each stand of trees. He confirms the species of trees, the density or frequency of the trees, and then age, size, and growing condition. He determines whether or not the trees have been stunted or damaged - and the type of site the trees are growing on. Is it a dry site or a moist cove? Is it south facing or north facing? Is it high on the slope, mid-slope, or further down the hill or mountain? And so forth.

The tools the forester carries with him are an increment borer, which he uses to determine the age of a tree; a clinometer, to get the height; and a wedge prism, which he uses to measure the density or frequency of trees in a given area.

After the forester has finished his measurements, he then averages his sample points to determine the overall condition of the entire stand of trees. With this information, he can then prescribe a treatment for that particular area. Generally, if the stand is mature or in a poor growing condition, it qualifies for a timber harvest – often a clearcut followed by replanting or natural regeneration to get the area growing with healthy young seedlings once again. If the stand is overstocked or too dense, but is otherwise growing well, it may qualify for some type of thinning to give the remaining trees the necessary sunlight and room to grow at optimum capability.

Again, I want to emphasize that this procedure gives us only the basic information necessary to determine where we cut our timber. Many other factors such as accessibility, economic feasibility, and environmental protection play a large role in our decisions as to where we cut. But by having this basic silvicultural data, we can plan our harvest areas in a systematic way, in order to ensure that our nation has a continuous supply of the products our forests can produce - wood, water, wildlife, forage, and recreation.

February 22, 1979 –

Forestry in the United States is a relatively new profession when compared to other countries, especially certain European countries. Forestry did not really begin to take shape here until the early 1900's. In spite of this fact, rules and regulations pertaining to Forestry have been with us since the days of our first colonists.

From time to time I'll provide short historical sketches about these early days in American Forestry. Today - **The Colonial Period (1600-1777):**

When the earliest settlers landed on American shores, forests covered nearly all of the land from the eastern seaboard to the Great Plains. Wood was abundant and free for the taking. The colonial period was characterized by a gradual pushing back of the forests to make room for settlement.

Because transportation facilities were poor, local wood shortages sometimes arose near the larger towns, and these occasionally led to restrictions on cutting. But most people felt, in the words of Gifford Pinchot, that "the thing to do with the forest was to get rid of it." (Pinchot is widely recognized as the father of the U.S. Forest Service, serving as the agency's first Chief. His vision and leadership influenced much of the early forestry in the United States.)

Here are some of the earliest forestry-related laws on record:

1626 - Plymouth Colony passed an ordinance prohibiting cutting timber on colony lands without official consent.

1681 - William Penn's ordinance for the Pennsylvania colony required that, in clearing land, settlers leave one acre in trees for every five acres cleared. This provision was not enforced for very long.

1691 – The Massachusetts colony charter reserved to the King of England, to provide masts for the British Navy, all white pine trees two feet thick or more (at one foot above the ground) growing on land not previously granted to a private person. Later similar provisions applied from Maine to New Jersey. Violators were tried in admiralty courts and punished severely.

1710 - The first community forest in the United States was established at Newington, NH. The 110-acre forest owned by the town has since yielded continuing benefits to the community for more than two centuries, helping to build the village church, parsonage, town hall, and library; furnishing planks for bridges; and fuel to heat public buildings.

1728 - British Navigation Acts prohibited the colonies from shipping "naval stores" products - pitch, tar, and crude gum - direct to foreign countries. Measures for the regulation of the naval stores industry and for the payment of bounties were introduced by the Royal Governor of North Carolina.

1760 - Another of America's earliest community forests was established at Danville, NH. A committee was appointed to manage the town's 75-acre woodland "to keep the parson warm." Over the years the forest has yielded some $10,000 worth of products.

1777 - North Carolina law prohibited unlawful "firing" of the woods and declared that forest fires are extremely destructive to the soil.

March 1, 1979 –

This week's article was written by Debbie Day, Manpower Coordinator for both the Blairsville and Dahlonega Ranger Districts. Debbie is a native of Atlanta and attended Antioch College near Springfield, Ohio. She taught high school for two years in Atlanta and elementary school for two years in Blairsville prior to her job with the Forest Service, which began in January 1978. During the summers of 1976 and 1977, Debbie was summer Camp Director for our Youth Conservation Corps (YCC) Camp that we housed at Young Harris College.

Note: *The overall term for our human resource programs, particularly in the 1970s and 1980s, and which included the Senior Citizen program, our youth programs, and* *others, was the Manpower Program. We certainly employed a large number of females, in addition to males, but Manpower Program was the official designation and language of that time. Now for Debbie's column:*

The Forest Service was originally established to manage our nation's natural resources, but recently we have extended our function to help develop another important resource -- people. To better manage our natural resources, we found an increasing need for more manpower. In return, the benefits to people through productive employment, training, and experience have proven invaluable.

Presently the Brasstown Ranger District is operating four manpower programs: the Senior Citizen Employment Program, the Young Adult Conservation Corps; the Youth Conservation Corps; and the Forest Service Volunteer Program. Although each program is unique, all were developed with the basic idea of bringing human and natural resources together to the benefit of both.

As our society has changed, it has become increasingly difficult for older people to find productive and challenging jobs. To help, Congress passed the Older American Act, which established the Senior Conservation Employment Program (SCEP). It is a cooperative program within the

Department of Labor designed for senior citizens, primarily in rural areas.

The SCEP seeks to provide a supplemental income for senior citizens; demonstrate and utilize their skills, experience, and wisdom; and provide work experience and training that will encourage and help employers to hire more senior workers. The Brasstown Ranger District has participated in this program since 1970.

Another problem our country faces is the unemployment of our youth. In 1976 the highest rate of unemployment was found in the 16 to 23 age bracket. Congress passed Public Law 95-93 to establish the Young Adult Conservation Corps (YACC). This program provides a year of productive employment for young men and women, ages 16 through 23, in conservation work on public lands. YACC is administered jointly by the U.S. Departments of Labor, Agriculture, and Interior.

A little over a year ago the Brasstown Ranger District began its first YACC program. Already we have employed 26 young people from Towns and Union Counties. The cost of the local program last year was $78,114, while the appraised value of the accomplished work was $145,818. A 187% return on our tax dollars is certainly good news to the taxpayer in this day and time.

Another program aimed at our nation's young people is the Youth Conservation Corps (YCC). Public Law 93-408 established YCC within the Departments of Interior and Agriculture to meet three objectives: 1. To provide gainful employment of America's youths, ages 15 through 18, during the summer months in a healthful outdoor atmosphere; 2. To provide an opportunity for understanding and appreciating the nation's natural environment and heritage; 3. To further develop and maintain the natural resources of the United States by the youths who will ultimately be responsible for maintaining and managing these resources for the American people.

YCC began on the Brasstown Ranger District five years ago. We operate a residential program that has enrolled youths from all over Georgia. Competition for the few slots has been keen due to the success and fine reputation this unique work/study program has earned.

The fourth manpower program, the Forest Service Volunteers, was established by Congress in 1972 to enable interested citizens to assist in the important conservation work of the Forest Service. Anyone, young, old and in between, who wants to become involved may apply. Volunteers are limited only by their willingness to serve.

For the past two summers the Brasstown Ranger District has benefited from having a volunteer as a Campground Host at Lake Winfield Scott. This summer, we plan to expand our program and use volunteers at Brasstown Bald, Lake Chatuge campground, and as house parents in our YCC program. These volunteers have allowed us to expand and improve our service to the public.

Natural Resources -- Human Resources ... a natural bridge for the betterment of both.

Ranger's Notebook - Forest Service manpower programs date back to 1933 when the Civilian Conservation Corps (CCC) was formed. The first camp, Camp Roosevelt, was located on the George Washington National Forest near Luray, Virginia. The CCC camps operated until 1942 and employed over 2 million young men who accomplished a vast amount of forestry, conservation, and natural resource work in this country.

March 8, 1979 –

Spring is in the air! Though I'm sure Ol' Man Winter won't go away without a couple of more chilly blasts, we've at least had enough of a glimpse at springtime to ease our "cabin fever" somewhat. It won't be long until we'll see the redbud and dogwood trees blooming. And I've already heard several birds singing on warmer mornings. Yessirree! Spring is just around the corner.

There's much beauty to behold during the Winter, but the coming of Spring seems to bring a certain joy to everyone's heart. The changing seasons – how lucky we are to be able to enjoy each one of them in its own special way.

Besides bringing warmer temperatures, longer days, animal activity, and baseball season, Spring also brings something that is dear to my heart – the emergence in our forests of the tasty, delectable, wild ramp. This small plant with the green top and the onion-like stem is one of the pure delights of Springtime.

The ramp is found growing throughout the Appalachian Mountains, primarily in moist, shaded coves and in rich soil. Its green leaves are among the first to emerge from the forest floor after the long Winter. Young, tender ramps are the best ones to eat and these can be found from mid-April to early June, depending upon what state you happen to live in. Much later than that, and the ramps become tough.

Being a native of the West Virginia mountains, I was introduced to ramps at an early age. Other than cornbread mixed with buttermilk, there's nothing my Dad would rather eat than ramps. Like father, like son.

A side benefit of eating ramps is that they are very high in vitamin C. This was very important to early mountain people because of the lack of vitamin C foods in the Springtime.

Don't let anyone talk you into not eating ramps because of their supposedly strong taste or because their smell lingers on your breath somewhat longer than normal onions. In short, if you like onions of any kind or prepared in any manner, then you'll like ramps. This is because the ramp is a cook's delight, since it is such a versatile food.

If you like raw onions, then you'll love ramps. Eat them with bread and butter; sprinkle them with salt; or try them my favorite way – with cornbread and beans. Do you like French-fried onion rings? Great! Just cut off the leaves of your ramps, dip the stems in batter, and throw them in the deep fryer – presto! French fried ramps. This also takes a little of the nippiness out of their taste for those who don't like them raw. My wife won't eat them raw, but French fried and dipped in ketchup – Um-umh. My dad's uncle liked ramps any way you could think of, but I always remember his wife deep frying them when I was around.

Other ways to prepare them? Take the tops that you just cut off and cook them like greens, If you desire, add vinegar. Mighty tasty! How about with scrambled eggs? Cut the ramps (tops and bottoms) into small pieces and scramble them in your eggs. What a delicious breakfast. Chop them up and add them to your tossed salad or fry them whole in bacon grease. These are only a few of the more popular ways to prepare ramps. If you have a favorite way to fix them that I haven't mentioned here, please let me know. I'd love to try it.

Ranger's Notebook – Along with ramps, Spring also brings the opening of Brasstown Bald Visitor Center. We open for "weekends – only" on Saturday, March 10th. This continues through the end of April, at which time we begin our daily operations.

March 15, 1979 –

In one of my previous columns, I discussed the development of the profession of Forestry during America's Colonial Period. Today, I'll continue the series with some forestry-related happenings that occurred between the time of our country's independence and the Civil War.

The Young Republic

In the first century of American independence, settlement spread over most of the country. The forests were drawn upon heavily to create new farms, to supply the growing industries, to extend the railroad lines, and to build the many new towns and cities that sprang up. This was a period of forest exploitation, gradual at first, but rapidly increasing after about 1850. Only a few concerned citizens were beginning to think about the future of the forests.

1799 – The Federal Timber Purchases Act appropriated $200,000 to buy timber and timberland for naval purposes, an early recognition of the need for conserving timber supplies. Blackbeard's and Grover's Islands off the Georgia coast were purchased.

1822 – An act for "the preservation of timber of the United States in Florida" was passed to prevent the destruction and theft of government timber.

1827 – The Federal Timber Reservation Act established the Santa Rosa Live Oak Timber Reserve in Florida for the Navy, the first reservation of public land for timber supplies.

1828 – Santa Rosa, a peninsula jutting into the Bay of Pensacola, Florida, was intended to be our first forest experiment station. It contained 30,000 acres. Live oaks and live oak acorns were planted, brush was cleared, fire lanes were opened, selective cutting was done, and trespassers were kept out. Plans were made to make the forest pay for itself in forest products. Unfortunately, the forest became a controversial political issue and work was ordered dropped after just two years.

1830 – Missouri's forest cultivation petition asked Congress for a township for experiments in raising forest timber.

1831 – The Timber Trespass Act, related to live oak and other timber, became the basis for the present-day law for the prevention of timber trespass on government land.

1837 – The Massachusetts Legislature authorized a survey of forest conditions, with a view to inducing landowners to consider the importance of "continuing, improving, and enlarging the forests of the state."

1844 – The New York Association for the Protection of Game, one of the earliest wildlife conservation organizations, was founded.

1849 – The U.S. Department of Interior was created.

1850 – The first federal timber agents were appointed by the Secretary of Interior to protect public timberlands. The agents were discontinued in 1855 and their duties were added to the District Land Registers and Receivers.

1851 – Utah law limited timber cutting in Great Salt Lake County, with a $100 fine for anyone who wasted, burned, or otherwise destroyed timber.

1858 – The Southern Pine Petition, from the Georgia Legislature, asked Congress to appoint a federal commission to inquire into the extent and duration of the southern pine belt.

1860 – "Forest Trees of North America," a 30-page section of the annual report of the Agricultural Division of the Patent Office, was issued. It listed the kinds of trees found here and discussed their effects on soil, climate, and health.

1862 – The U.S. Department of Agriculture was created. The Homestead Act was passed.

March 22, 1979 –

Last week Frances Mason and I presented a short program to the third grade children from Union County Elementary School. It's a real pleasure to get a chance to talk to these kids. They give you their full attention and they're so very interested in everything you have to say.

Anyway, we showed them a movie called "The South's Amazing Forest," which tells about the role that forestry plays in the lives of southern people, the many types and uses of forest products, and how important it is to manage and protect our forests. We also talked about fire prevention and handed out some Smokey Bear materials. The kids loved the items – pencils, rulers, coloring sheets, and comic books. And there were larger posters for the teachers to place in their classrooms.

Two things stood out to me during the session. First, the children were very well behaved. This is a tribute to their fine teachers – Mrs. Akins, Mrs. Cook, Mrs. Gooch, and Mrs. Adams. Secondly, these kids are sharp! They asked a lot of pertinent and intelligent questions that we had to think about for a few seconds before answering. One thing for sure –

third graders today know a lot more than I did when I was their age.

On another note, Spring fire season is here. I urge everyone to be careful with their trash fires and debris burning.

We've brought in a helicopter and three men from western National Forests to assist us in our firefighting efforts. The pilot is Monty Montgomery from the Wasatch National Forest, which is headquartered in Salt Lake City, Utah. The helicopter foreman is Lloyd Whitaker from Missoula, Montana. The helitack crew is composed of three local men from our District – Danny Owenby, Zane Rogers, and Milton Bradley. The final link to this fine crew is the fuel truck driver, Steve Heilberger, who also works out of Salt Lake City. These six fellows are real professionals and they certainly enhance our firefighting capabilities. Next week, I'll detail a little more about this operation.

Employee Spotlight - I'm sure most readers recognize the name, L.A. Rich. Or maybe you know him personally. L.A. is one of the important cornerstones of our operations here on the Brasstown Ranger District of the Chattahoochee National Forest. He was born and raised in Union County and began working with the U.S. Forest Service in 1955. He's done everything from planting pines and running land lines to manning fire towers and marking timber. His present position is the District Timber Sales Administrator. He's usually in charge of five to ten timber sales, but told me he once had 18 going at the same time. His knowledge and dedicated work help keep our timber program running efficiently. L.A., his wife Mabel, and one son live just outside of Blairsville on the Young Harris Highway.

March 29, 1979 –

This Spring's fire season on the Brasstown Ranger District has brought with it a slight change in the way we operate. We still depend upon our highly skilled and trained District crews to do the bulk of the work in fighting wildfires. And we still use airplanes to assist us with our fire detection efforts. The change is that we now have a helicopter and crew on duty to complement our fire suppression crews.

As I mentioned last week, the helicopter crew consists of six men – a pilot, a foreman, a three-man attack crew, and a fuel truck driver, who performs support duties. The pilot, Monty

Montgomery, and the fuel truck driver, Steve Heilberger, are from the U.S. Forest Service office in Salt Lake City, Utah. The helicopter foreman, Lloyd Whitaker, is a Forest Service employee from Missoula, Montana. These three men are on loan to us here on the Chattahoochee National Forest. The three-man attack crew consists of local Brasstown Ranger District firefighters – Danny Owenby, Zane Rogers, and Milton Bradley, who are highly trained and in excellent physical condition.

The three western fire personnel have worked on fires all over the country and are a big asset to us. While here, when they have down time, they're helping to train some of our local personnel in the uses of a helicopter in fighting wildfires. By the way, Steve made me promise to mention that he is a Utah transplant, originally from New York state.

We're finding the helicopter to be beneficial in several ways. First, in many cases the helicopter can deliver four men to an ongoing wildfire very rapidly. They can either put out the fire, if possible, or at least get a good jump on things before the ground forces arrive. Two weeks ago our crew flew to Doogen Mountain near Chatsworth to help out our Forest Service personnel over there. They actually put a line around the fire before the ground forces arrived.

Secondly, after the pilot delivers the crew, he can begin to locate and dump water on the fire with his bucket attachment. He can hit the head of the fire and thereby slow its rate of spread, so that the ground crews can get a line around the fire quicker. Thirdly, after the fire is controlled the pilot can dump water on any hot spots, such as burning snags or stumps. This is particularly beneficial when we're fighting a fire high on a mountain top with no water readily available for our ground crews to use for "mop-up" operations.

And fourthly, the helicopter can ferry tools and supplies to ground crews faster and easier than people on foot. This is extremely beneficial during emergency situations. There are other uses of the helicopter, but these are four of the most important.

Ground crews will continue to be the backbone of our firefighting efforts. You cannot put out a fire entirely from the air. But the helicopter, used in conjunction with ground forces, is a valuable tool indeed.

As the Assistant District Ranger responsible for the fire program, I have gotten to know and work closely with Monty and his crew. It has been an enjoyable and educational experience – even a few of the helicopter rides Monty gave me enroute to heli-spots out on the District. These heli-spots are cleared areas located out in the forest, where the helitack crew will wait on standby duty, to allow for quicker and easier access to wildfires once they occur. As a former fixed-wing airplane pilot, I have never been completely comfortable in a helicopter, especially flying not far above treetop level like we did recently. But Monty's ability and professionalism put me at ease. (I still prefer flying in planes, rather than helicopters though).

Ranger's Notebook – In the Fall of 1871, the Peshtigo Forest Fire in Wisconsin burned over one million acres, including the entire town of Peshtigo, and caused the deaths of 1500 people. The heat was so severe that it was reported that dead fish floated on all the rivers, and birds in flight were overcome and fell to the ground.

April 4, 1979 –

There are 187 million acres of National Forest land in the United States, including Puerto Rico. This includes land in every state except Iowa, Maryland, Delaware, New Jersey, Connecticut, Rhode Island, and Massachusetts. Ownership of these lands is vested with the approximately 219 million citizens of this country. That figures out to be just over 4/5 of an acre per person.

If you had your say, how would you want the Forest Service to manage your 4/5 of an acre?

Or, how would you want all of the 187 million acres of National Forests managed?

More realistically, how would you like to see your favorite National Forest managed? This could be the Chattahoochee in Georgia, the Nantahala in North Carolina, the Sumter in South Carolina, or the Cherokee in Tennessee. Or you might have some particular interest in the Ocala National Forest in Florida, the Bitterroot in Montana, or the Allegheny in Pennsylvania.

The 187 million acres of National Forests represent a treasury of many things. The American people use these forests for camping, hiking, fishing, hunting, watershed protection, grazing, timber production, wilderness, wildlife habitat, and many other important things.

Which, and how much, of the desired products and uses these lands will supply must be planned for and determined well ahead of time. Forests cannot be hurried. Thus, each National Forest will be preparing a Land Management Plan, which will outline how the Forest will be managed over a 10 or 15 year period.

These Plans are required by the National Forest Management Act, which Congress passed in 1976. Early thoughts are that Georgia's Chattahoochee and Oconee National Forest Plans will be completed no later than 1985, possibly sooner.

If you have thoughts and opinions on the decisions to be made about the National Forests, contact any Forest Service office to express your ideas or concerns. This is important because the results could affect you personally for many years to come.

Employee Spotlight – Betty Taylor has worked for the U.S. Forest Service since June 14, 1965. She worked on the Toccoa Ranger District in Blue Ridge for her first two years. She then transferred to Blairsville and has been here ever since.

Betty is responsible for all clerical duties on the District, which includes such things as budgeting, purchasing supplies and materials, maintaining personnel records, supervising receptionists and other office workers, and so many other things that I can't list them all here.

Betty works indoors most of the time, with occasional trips to places like our Supervisor's Office in Gainesville for meetings and training sessions. The one training session she remembers most was held in New Orleans, Louisiana and included a tour of the huge National Finance Center located there.

Betty is a storehouse of knowledge on all aspects of Forest Service operations and is appreciated very much by all of her co-workers. She is married, has two daughters, and lives on the Blue Ridge Highway.

April 11, 1979 –

Odds and Ends from the Forest Service –

*In October 1924, the area which is now the Fort Benning Military Reservation at Columbus, Georgia was designated as a National Forest. However, in December 1927, it was given to the military and has become one of this nation's most important defense installations.

*In a similar manner, much of the current Eglin Air Force Base in Florida was a National Forest until the outbreak of World War II in Europe, when a proving ground for aircraft armament was established at Eglin. The U.S. Forest Service ceded over 340,000 acres of the Choctawhatchee National Forest to the War Department on October 18, 1940.

*In the late 1800's and early 1900's, deer were just about hunted to the point of elimination in north Georgia. The famous Ranger Woody began bringing deer to Georgia from the Pisgah National Forest in North Carolina during the mid-1920's. The first managed deer hunt was held from October 2 – November 29, 1940. Presently, the deer herd is well established in north Georgia and, under professional management, it will continue to thrive.

*The highest peak in the Appalachian Mountains is Mount Mitchell in North Carolina. This is also the highest point east of the Rockies, rising to an elevation of 6,684 feet. In comparison, Brasstown Bald, the highest point in Georgia is 4,784 feet above sea level.

*The native fir trees that occur in the Southern Appalachian Mountains (North Carolina, Tennessee, Virginia) are often mistakenly called balsam fir. In fact, though, this southern tree is only a cousin to balsam and it is a completely separate species. Its true name is Fraser fir and it is one of the favorite Christmas tree species for many people.

Historically, Fraser fir is also said to have occurred in extreme southern West Virginia, the far northwest part of South Carolina, and yes, in the mountains of north Georgia, near the North Carolina border.

*It is also interesting to note that while balsam fir is primarily a tree found in Canada and several of our northern states, the southernmost known occurrence of balsam fir is found on the Monongahela National Forest, high in the mountains of eastern West Virginia. I have actually walked among those trees when I worked at the Monongahela National Forest in the early 1970's. I was born near that area and my dad and his friends growing up referred to the balsam fir by its local name, "blister pine." This was because of the small pockets or "blisters" of sticky resin located on the bark of the tree.

*The red spruce occurs both in northern and southern mountain forests. It can be found from southeastern Canada and New England all the way south to Tennessee and North Carolina. I suspect, and it has been historically mentioned, that a few red spruce trees have grown (and a few may still be growing) on the highest mountains of northeast Georgia right along the North Carolina border.

Ranger's Notebook – On March 1, 1966 the
U.S. Treasury received the two-billionth (is that
a word?) dollar of National Forest receipts
from the Forest Service. Those receipts come
primarily from timber sales, grazing fees,
mineral royalties, recreation fees, and other
fees for rights-of-way and other special uses.

April 18, 1979 –

*Today's article was written by
Ron Mize, who is a Zone Wildlife
Biologist stationed at the Chattooga
Ranger District in Clarkesville,
Georgia. Ron has wildlife management
responsibilities on the Chattahoochee
National Forest's four easternmost
Districts, managed out of Clarkesville,
Clayton, Blairsville, and Dahlonega. He
has been working on the Chattahoochee
for two years.*

*Ron is a native of east Texas and
received his degree in wildlife biology
from Texas A&M University. He is
presently working toward a graduate
degree in the area of timber/wildlife
coordination. Prior to working for the
Forest Service, Ron served for two and*

one-half years as a civilian Forester at Eglin Air Force Base in Florida.

Wildlife Management on Southern National Forests

Beginning in 1971, the "featured species" concept of wildlife management was implemented on the southern national forests. According to the Multiple Use and Sustained Yield Act of 1960, national forest lands must be managed to produce continued and sustained yields of wildlife, timber, water, forage, and outdoor recreation. The featured species concept guides wildlife habitat management within this framework.

Under this concept the Forest Service, in partnership with the appropriate state Fish and Game agencies and with public input, selects featured wildlife species for various units of forest land. Selections are made with input from other program managers and include considerations for the size of the land unit and what types of tree species are present. In the planning phase four major items are considered: habitat capability; compatibility with other resources; public interest and needs; and partner and public input.

After the featured species has been selected, its habitat requirements are used to help make management decisions, such as coordination with timber activities, planting needs, and so forth. Timber management activities, for instance, may be modified as to size, location, timing of the harvest, etc. depending upon the species being featured – deer, grouse, turkeys, non-game species, and so on. Adequate up-front environmental analysis is made to ensure that decisions are correct.

In addition to size, location, and timing of timber harvests, other considerations include: will the site be converted to pine after the harvest or naturally regenerated to hardwoods; what other types of tree species are in the surrounding areas for food, cover, and dens/nests; what types of site preparation will be done after a timber harvest; what are the ages of the harvested stand and adjacent areas; is prescribed burning appropriate either before or after the harvest; what kinds of seeding on roads and skid trails can benefit the wildlife species.

Though there may be "featured" species in an area, many other wildlife species also benefit from the forest management activities. The goals of both forestry and wildlife are very compatible. A mix of tree size classes and age classes creates a diversity that is beneficial to both wildlife and forestry. Habitat ranging from clearcuts to mature sawtimber and everything in between – seedlings and saplings; pole size trees; immature sawtimber – creates an ideal overall habitat for diverse wildlife populations.

The southern National Forests are committed to considering wildlife needs as part of the overall timber management program.

Ranger's Notebook – The Biological Survey in the U.S. Department of Agriculture, which had begun as the Division of Economic Ornithology and Mammalogy in 1885, later became the U.S. Fish and Wildlife Service in 1940 and was reassigned to the U.S. Department of Interior, where it remains today. Cooperation with the Forest Service has been close, due to the relationship between forest management and wildlife management.

April 26, 1979 –

Recently we hosted a field trip that involved personnel from all Districts on the Forest. It was an educational field trip that dealt with hardwood silviculture. Silviculture is the science of managing and caring for the trees in a forest. It includes establishing the young seedlings; controlling species composition within the timber stands; maintaining the trees in a healthy condition throughout their life so as to optimize growth; eventually harvesting the mature timber stands; and preparing the site for a new crop of trees.

When I mention hardwoods, I'm referring to trees that lose their leaves in the Fall and not necessarily to how hard the wood actually is. The pines that keep their needles year round are commonly referred to by Foresters as softwoods. Some hardwood trees, such as basswood and yellow poplar, actually have wood that is soft; and some softwood trees actually have wood that is hard. It's a little bit confusing, but the thing to remember is that hardwoods lose their leaves in the Fall and softwoods keep their needles year round.

Now, back to the field trip. The expertise for the session was provided by two research scientists: Don Beck, from the Southeastern Forest Experiment Station in Asheville, North Carolina; and Martin Dale, from the Northeastern Forest Experiment Station in Delaware, Ohio. The emphasis of the session was on: 1) controlling the species composition of young stands; and 2) thinning of stands throughout their life in order to increase the growth on the remaining trees.

One problem foresters are experiencing is that after we cut or harvest our oak stands, we are not getting as much young oak in the new stands. We would like to see as much or more oak regenerate in the new stands because oak is valuable from both a timber and a wildlife standpoint. So, these researchers are studying ways to maintain a high percentage of oaks in our future forests.

Some of the research studies include: 1) using controlled fires to help get rid of unwanted tree species and to help establish desirable species (oaks); 2) pre-harvest treatments to help establish advanced oak reproduction. If there are lots of young, healthy oak saplings present in the stand before the mature trees are cut, they can usually compete with other fast growing tree species that seed-in after a harvest; and 3) using herbicides to get rid of unwanted tree species.

The other main item discussed during the field trip was the thinning of immature stands of trees. If trees are left to grow in a crowded condition, when they reach a mature age, they aren't as large as they could be. But if some of the poorer quality trees are "thinned out" over the years, when the stand reaches maturity the remaining trees are bigger and of higher quality. By thinning, you maintain the health and vigor of the remaining trees, while also being able to utilize the wood from the trees you cut.

Research in hardwood silviculture will provide answers and give us recommendations to help manage our forests more effectively to help meet the ever increasing demands placed upon them.

Employee Spotlight – Jessie King is a lifelong resident of Union County, who began working for the U.S. Forest Service in 1957. Prior to that, he spent five years in the U.S. Army. Jessie is one of the mainstays of our recreation program and most people know him for the fine work he does at our Brasstown Bald Visitor Center. Over the years, he has marked timber, helped survey boundary lines, flagged out road locations, planted trees, and worked in a fire tower, among numerous other duties. There aren't many Forest Service jobs that Jessie hasn't been involved with over the years. Now he works primarily in recreation, visitor information, law enforcement, and fire prevention. Jessie and his wife, Rosa, live on the Pat Colwell Road.

<u>**May 3, 1979 –**</u>

Forest roads are a familiar sight to anyone visiting the Chattahoochee National Forest. The roads are part of a transportation system that is necessary to provide access for forest users and forest managers. Roads serve a variety of purposes ranging from timber hauling and sightseeing to recreation area access and fire control.

The standard of these roads varies according to the type of use each one receives. For instance, there are high standard, paved roads like the Richard Russell Scenic Highway; and on the other end of the scale are short, temporary roads that are used to bring logs to a central landing area to be loaded on to log trucks and hauled to the mill.

The number of roads needed in a forest varies according to management activities and use patterns. And, of course, some people think we should have more roads, while others think we should have fewer roads.

Despite differences of opinion as to the standard of roads needed and how many there should be, two things stand out. First, intensive, multiple-use forest management requires a certain number of roads; and secondly, all road construction and maintenance brings the potential for soil erosion and stream sedimentation.

The percentage of soil erosion occurring in the United States as a result of forest management activities is a very small part of the total. National statistics show that most soil erosion comes from farming, followed by such activities as runoff from housing developments and shopping centers; new construction; and road banks along the highway system throughout the country. However, this doesn't mean that soil and water considerations are unimportant in forest management. They're very important indeed!

The main cause of soil erosion and stream siltation in forestry-related work is roads. It is a common misconception that clearcutting causes soil erosion. That is totally false. Soil must be bared for erosion to occur and cutting a tree does not bare any soil. The roads built to remove the trees from the woods, however, can cause soil erosion.

Since roads offer the greatest potential for soil erosion in forest management, and since we know that some roads are going to be necessary, we concentrate our soil and water protection efforts on proper road location, construction, and maintenance.

These are some of the things we consider when planning our roads:

1) Stay away from unstable soils, steep slopes, and springs or wet, boggy areas.
2) Locate roads as far away from streams as possible.
3) If stream crossings are necessary, cross them at right angles using culverts and/or bridges.
4) Limit roads to the minimum mileage needed.
5) Quickly re-seed disturbed soils along road banks, or whenever roads will be closed permanently.
6) Leave buffer strips of vegetation between roads and streams to serve as sediment traps.
7) Perform regular maintenance on permanent roads.
8) Adequate surfacing, such as gravel, should be used on logging haul roads.
9) Since many roads are not constructed for all-weather use, close them during off-season periods.

A properly located, constructed and maintained forest road will result in few environmental problems and is likely to have lower maintenance costs in the long run.

Ranger's Notebook – Timber production has played a major role in the growth and development of the United States. It has been estimated that 2,400,000 million board feet of lumber were cut between 1776 and World War II. That was enough to build 52,000,000 urban homes; 12,000,000 farm houses; 2,000,000 schools and libraries; 650,000 churches; and 450,000 factories.

May 10, 1979 –

Want to help celebrate a birthday in a unique way? All Americans will have the chance to do so in 1980.

In recognition of next year's 75th anniversary of the U.S. Forest Service, there will be a national campaign called "Plant a Birthday Tree." The purpose of the campaign is to celebrate our 75th anniversary by planting 75 million more trees in 1980 than we planted in 1979. President Carter is being requested to declare 1980 as the "Year of the Tree" in honor of the anniversary. Every citizen will be encouraged to plant a tree in honor of their own birthdays, family members' birthdays, anniversaries, or to commemorate other significant events.

The campaign should help to increase everyone's appreciation of trees and forestry, as well as to create a greater awareness of the Forest Service role in managing our nation's natural resources.

Additional information on the "Plant a Birthday Tree" campaign will be made available during the next few months.

On another note, let's mention the Forestry Incentives Program (FIP). This is a cost-share program for private forest landowners that was authorized by Congress in 1973. The FIP is a program of the U.S. Department of Agriculture, the Forest Service's parent agency, and day-to-day administration is handled by the Agricultural Stabilization and Conservation Service (ASCS).

Here's how it works. Landowners can get financial help for forestry if:

1) They own between 10 and 1,000 acres of land.
2) They are not in a business of manufacturing wood products.
3) Their land is suitable for growing trees; planting or seeding to a new stand of trees; producing marketable timber crops; and continued forest management.

Landowners can actually get money to:
1) Plant trees.
2) Improve their woodlands by thinning, pruning, releasing young trees, or site preparation.

Interested landowners should contact their local ASCS office, which will work with the state forestry agency to examine the property; approve the forestry practice requested; and develop a management plan, which is worked out with the owner.

The FIP is open to all eligible landowners. The federal share of the costs ranges up to 75 percent, varying by state and county. Landowners can enter into long-term agreements which run from three to five years. Maximum payment is $10,000 in any one year.

If you're interested, maybe the FIP can help you put your idle acres to work.

Ranger's Notebook – This Spring on the Brasstown Ranger District, we planted 95,000 trees covering 525 acres. Species planted were white pine and loblolly pine.

May 16, 1979 –

The following notes of interest concerning Brasstown Bald Mountain are taken from a publication we have here at the office, covering the history of the Chattahoochee National Forest. From time to time, I'll run excerpts of this history that might be of interest to residents of Towns and Union counties.

They very top of the mountain is located in Land Lot 274, District 17, Section 1, of the original Cherokee County. Now, the Towns and Union county line splits the top of the mountain.

Most of the mountain and the adjoining acres were purchased by the federal government from Pfister and Vogel Leather Company of Milwaukee, Wisconsin. That portion of the mountain top consisting of approximately ½ acre and enclosed by the present paved highway was donated to the federal government by the State of Georgia on May 27, 1947. Title was accepted on June 29, 1949. The last private tract of one acre near the current parking lot was acquired by exchange with the State of Georgia on December 23, 1955.

Brasstown Bald is the highest point in Georgia with an elevation of 4,784 feet above sea level. The name is derived from the Cherokee Indian words *Itse'yi*, meaning "new green place" or "place of fresh green;" and *Itse'hi* meaning "green or unripe vegetation." These words were commonly used to refer to a tract of ground made green by fresh growing vegetation after having been cleared of timber or having been burned over.

A name occurring in several places in the old Cherokee country was variously written as Echia, Echoee, Etchowee, and sometimes written as "Brasstown," from confusing the previously mentioned word *Itse'yi* with *untsaiyi*, which meant "brass."

Settlements called Brasstown occurred along Brasstown Creek of the Tugaloo River in Oconee County, South Carolina; on the Little Tennessee River near Franklin, Macon County, North Carolina near the junction of Cartoogaja Creek; and on the upper Brasstown Creek of the Hiawassee River directly north of Brasstown Bald.

The Brasstown Ranger District contains one of the first tracts of land purchased in the United States under the Weeks Law for flood control purposes. In 1912, Andrew and N.W. Gennett of Asheville, North Carolina sold to the

Forest Service 32,000 acres of land for $220,626.22. These types of purchases began the building of the National Forests in the eastern United States.

Ranger's Notebook — In 1934 the Eastern Region of the U.S. Forest Service was divided and a new Region, the Southern, was created with headquarters in Atlanta, Georgia. The current Southern Region - Region 8 - includes national forests in Virginia, Kentucky, Tennessee, North Carolina, Georgia, South Carolina, Florida, Alabama, Mississippi, Oklahoma, Arkansas, Texas, and Louisiana.

May 24, 1979 —

Today's article was written by a friend of mine, Al Vanderpoel, who is an Engineer with the U.S. Forest Service. Al is a native of Wisconsin and at the time of this writing worked on the Wayne National Forest in Ironton, Ohio. He is one of a large group of specialists who now work with Foresters in handling the complex land management activities on the National Forests of this country.

When you think of the Forest Service, naturally you think of Foresters. They sell the timber, run the campgrounds, manage the land, and comprise most of the supervisors. Foresters made up over 90 percent of the work force in the early years. They were a dedicated group who often worked alone and were in complete charge of the land assigned to them. Much of the early work involved inventorying the land, dealing with trespassers, surveying and mapping, and fighting forest fires. Over the years, as their jobs grew and changed, they needed more assistance.

In the last 50 years, management of the forests has evolved to include the need for specialists. New laws were passed, adding to the complexity of an already complex job. In addition to Foresters there is now the need for Engineers, Soil Scientists, Landscape Architects, Hydrologists, Geologists, Wildlife Biologists, and others. In fact, today over 50 percent of the professional work force is made up of people other than Foresters.

Foresters still form the backbone of the agency, along with the forestry technicians, working on timber sales, tree planting, timber stand improvement, firewood projects, silvicultural inventories, and much of the day to day operations, including the recreation activities and firefighting jobs. But when faced with complex issues, they now have a support group of specialists to gather input and advice from.

For instance, Soil Scientists can offer advice on anything from tree planting to road locations; Geologists provide input on the important mineral resources located below the ground; Engineers deal with building construction, road construction and maintenance, and culvert placement; Landscape Architects have design input on hiking trails, campgrounds, and new recreation facilities; Wildlife Biologists can help determine what is beneficial and what may be harmful to many bird and animal species; and Hydrologists work with Foresters when there is a need for stream crossings in road locations, for example.

There are also a host of others providing support to the whole organization, ranging from Accountants and Personnel Specialists to Purchasing Agents, Secretaries, and Payroll and Benefits Clerks.

As you can see, it is no longer the Forester standing alone. While the Forester remains the primary decision maker in most instances, today's complexities require the input of many specialists in order to perform the quality management that the public expects on our National Forests.

Ranger's Notebook – The first commemorative postage stamp honoring forest conservation was issued by the Post Office Department in 1958.

May 30, 1979 –

With school ending this week, we know that our heavy-use recreation season is just around the corner. Even with the uncertainty over gasoline supplies, we're expecting a very busy summer. We're geared up and ready to go at Brasstown Bald Visitor Center, Lake Chatuge Campground, and Lake Winfield Scott Campground.

Speaking of Lake Winfield Scott, that recreation area will be getting a new look over the next one to two years. The layout of the campground itself will be revised to improve its appearance and to better distribute the recreation users. A few projects have already been completed and many more are scheduled. Here are the highlights of our reconstruction and rehabilitation plan for Lake Winfield Scott:

1) The entire road system will be re-done. This will include new paving and relocation of some sections.

2) The entrance to the campground itself will be moved from the current location to a point approximately ¼ mile south on Highway 180. The present entrance is near a sharp curve in the road and at the end of a bridge. This safety problem will be corrected by the new entrance location.

3) New signs will be placed at the entrance and throughout the campground.

4) Just inside the entrance, future plans call for a new entry station. A little further in, there will be a dump station for sanitary disposal of wastes from trailers and campers.

5) The present entrance will be blocked off about 200 feet in, and this section will be used as a parking lot for fishermen. We'll build a new dock just below the present entry building where these fishermen can launch canoes and small boats.

6) There will be approximately 41 campsites in the new campground after the reconstruction, complete with new parking spurs, tent pads, and fire grates.

7) The old bath house at the swimming beach is currently being remodeled and modernized.
8) All old roads and campsites will be revegetated and re-seeded.
9) Future plans also call for an amphitheatre, which will feature a view out over the lake.

These and other items will improve the appearance of the campground and help us provide visitors with a more enjoyable recreation experience.

Employee Spotlight – Charles Mason has been one of the familiar faces on the Brasstown Ranger District for a long time. Charles grew up in Union County and started working for the Forest Service as a summer student in 1962. His first duties were in recreation maintenance, trail construction and maintenance, working on the chainsaw crew, and manning the old fire lookout tower on Rocky Top. His present assignments include timber marking, wildlife habitat work, firefighting, and work leader for the summer YCC crews. Charles, his wife Frances, and one daughter live on the Pat Colwell Road.

June 7, 1979 –

The eastern panther, or mountain lion, is thought by most people to be a thing of the past. Many even believe the animal is extinct. But evidence gathered in the last few years is so strong that it is very likely the big cat actually survived in the East and is, in fact, growing in numbers.

Some local oldtimers still living can probably remember seeing panthers in the mountains. At one time they were fairly common. But in the last 50 or 60 years the panther seemed to have disappeared. The occasional sightings and reports were passed off as either someone's wild imagination or possibly just a large bobcat.

Other names that mountain folks gave the panther, or mountain lion, were catamount (for cat of the mountains), big cat, and "painter," a slang for panther. Throughout the Appalachian Mountains today, names like Big Cat Mountain, Painter Knob, Panther Creek, and Painter Run are quite common and point out that the big animal was once widespread in the East.

The strongest evidence to date of the eastern panther's existence comes from West Virginia. In that state the last reported killing of a panther had been in 1908. And although some people claimed the big cat still roamed the high, remote mountains, there was never any real proof – that is, until 1976.

In April of that year a farmer shot and killed a panther that was attacking his sheep in Pocahontas County, adjacent to the Monongahela National Forest. One week later, a pregnant panther was captured in the same county. It now resides at the state-run French Creek Game Farm near Buckhannon, West Virginia.

Though many people questioned where the animals actually came from, scientists who studied the two cats confirmed that they were, indeed, eastern mountain lions. And like they say, "a bird in the hand is worth two in the bush." Same goes for mountain lions. Proof positive now existed that the big cat still survived.

Are there panthers in the mountains of north Georgia? It's possible there are. There have been reports of sightings in Union, Towns, and Rabun counties. And these sightings are becoming more common throughout the eastern mountains – all the way from Canada to Georgia. Sightings have been made in Maine, New Hampshire, New York,

Pennsylvania, Virginia, West Virginia, North Carolina, and other states.

A hiker in New York's Adirondack Mountains took a picture, which seems to be authentic, of a panther he saw in the mountains. Closer home, sightings in the Great Smokey Mountains and near the Blue Ridge Parkway are being made frequently. A trails foreman in the Great Smokey Mountain National Park even saw a panther chasing a wild boar on the Appalachian Trail. So you can bet that there are a few panthers in north Georgia, too.

I like to think the animal still survives. If so, I'm glad. I'd hate to see the panther go the way of the passenger pigeon and other extinct animals.

If anyone sights a panther, it can be reported at our office. And better yet, if tracks are seen, especially in the snow, we will report this to a researcher who is stationed at Clemson University, over in South Carolina.

Whether or not you believe the big cat still roams the mountains, one thing is certain. There's enough believable evidence on hand to make you wonder.

Ranger's Notebook – The eastern mountain lion is protected under the Endangered Species

Act of 1973, which makes it illegal to hunt or kill the animal.

June 20, 1979 –

The Trackrock Gap Archaeological Area is the source of much local history and Indian folklore. We have a lot of information here at the office about Trackrock Gap, much of it collected by Harry Wright, who was District Ranger on the Brasstown District from 1951 – 1958.

The archaeological area consists of approximately 53 acres, lying on both sides of Trackrock Gap, one of the most important historical spots of the ancient Cherokee Nations. The micaceous soapstone rocks on both sides of the Gap are covered with petroglyphs of ancient Indian origin. It is from these markings, or tracks, that the Gap gets its name. The Cherokees called the place *Datsu'nalasgun'yl,* "where there are tracks," or *Degayelun'ha,* meaning "printed or branded place." The carvings are many and varied. Some of them resemble animal and bird tracks, while others resemble crosses, circles, and human footprints.

James Mooney, in his <u>Myths of the Cherokees</u>, which was printed in 1897-1898, gives many explanations for the origin of the carvings, which the Cherokees told to him during his many visits to their land after their removal to the Oklahoma Territory. The most sensible explanation advanced by Mooney is that the carvings were made by Indian hunters as they rested in the Gap. One myth is that Noah's Ark landed here and the many different kinds of animals left their footprints – a colorful story indeed.

The Reverend George White, in his <u>Historical Collections of Georgia</u>, written in 1855, mentions the Track Rock Gap carvings. He mentions a Dr. Stevenson, who wrote in 1834 about the vandalism that had occurred at the site. Stevenson himself admitted to cutting out some of the carvings and carrying them away.

Through the Gap ran an Indian trail older than recorded history. Mighty Cherokee warriors traveled through here on their way to do battle with their great enemy, the Creeks, who lived near the present day Marietta, Georgia and on south. Legends passed down tell of braves in full war regalia stopping to rest at the Gap and to drink the cool water from a nearby spring. Stories were told here about the greatness of the Cherokee nation.

At the time of the Jamestown settlement, the Cherokee nation included all of the state of Kentucky, most of Tennessee, and parts of Virginia, West Virginia, North Carolina, South Carolina, Georgia, and Alabama – an area of approximately 150,000 square miles. By the time of the American Revolution, the Cherokee nation had shrunk to about 40,000 square miles. At the time of the final cession, their area had been further reduced to roughly 10,000 square miles in Alabama, Georgia, North Carolina, and Tennessee. Trackrock was included in the final cession. (**Note:** the dictionary definition of "cession" is the act of giving up something - such as power, land, or rights - to another person, group, or country).

Stories tell of the Cherokees resting at Trackrock and gazing over the great valleys of the Nottely and Hiwassee Rivers. To the south stood Blood and Slaughter Mountains, where some of the bloodiest battles in Indian history took place between the Creeks and the Cherokees. To the north rose the high mountains of the Nantahala ranges, where Cherokee forefathers had lived for centuries.

Forests of hardwoods surrounded Trackrock gap and stories were told of great hunts in the area. And stories were told of the pretty Indian girls who came here to wait for the return of the warriors from their journeys.

One myth describes the Trackrock area as the residence of the Great Spirit, which greets non-Cherokee intruders with tremendous storms of thunder, lightning, and rain.

Ranger's Notebook — A "worked-out" corundum mine tunnels a long distance back into the mountain about 100 yards below the rocks on the south side of Trackrock Gap. During the late 1800s, corundum—a mineral second in hardness only to diamond—was mined extensively in north Georgia. Corundum was valuable in the manufacture of abrasives such as sandpaper. Impurities in the mineral also resulted in gem-quality sapphires and rubies.

June 27, 1979 —

This summer an eight-week Youth Conservation Corps (YCC) Camp is in residence at Young Harris College. The camp, a work-learning program hosted by the Brasstown District of the Chattahoochee National Forest, is directed by Skip Stewart, who contributed to this column.

YCC Camp Young Harris, which began June 17, is for youths 15 to 18 years of age. They apply for the program through their high school guidance counselors. This year 4,000 applications were received from throughout the state of Georgia. A computer randomly selected 18 girls and 16 boys for the Young Harris Camp. Stewart, who has previous experience with directing conservation camps, says that this group of students seems to be very conservation and environmentally oriented. "They want to work in the outdoors to help improve natural resources. That's YCC," he said.

The work is tough, but it needs to be done. Scheduled work this summer includes construction of two foot bridges on the High Shoals Trail; building a new trail around the Lake Chatuge Campground; rock wall repair work at Lake Winfield Scott; wildlife opening maintenance; erosion control projects; and civic projects at the Union County Recreation Center and at the Elementary School. Work supervisors for these projects are Charles Hughes, Sheldon Henderson, Charles Mason, and Ronnie Kelley, all Forest Service employees on the Brasstown Ranger District.

In addition to the regular work hours, YCC enrollees spend 10 hours per week on environmental education, under the guidance of our Camp Environmental Instructor, James Green. The activities include films, educational games, and environmental trips to various Forest Service locations, including a seed orchard and the Coweta Hydrologic Lab and Research facility in North Carolina, as well as the Young Harris College planetarium.

There are also recreation activities under the direction of counselors Liz Cornish, Dave Snow, Myrtle Figueras, and Curtis Hawkins. Activities include rafting, backpacking, swimming, volleyball, and various other group activities. An Outward Bound running activity was also completed in Franklin, North Carolina, led by counselor Liz Cornish.

Other staff members for the YCC Camp, serving as security guards and volunteer helpers, are Robert Edwards, Ruth Stager, and Bob Stager.

Stewart, who is a classroom teacher during the school year, really believes in the YCC program. "It's a total program," he says. "It gives youngsters a chance to grow in many capacities. These young men and women will take these experiences and skills they learned and apply them to their lives in ways which will make the YCC program investment worthwhile for many years to come," says Stewart.

July 5, 1979 –

The American chestnut tree was at one time perhaps the most valuable and widespread tree growing in the Appalachian Mountains, occurring from Alabama and Georgia all the way to Maine. The tree was highly prized for its nuts, which mountain people were able to sell for a profit, as well as use to supplement their own food supply. The nuts were also preferred by many species of wildlife; this was an important reason for the abundance of game in the mountains.

As far as the wood itself, there were so many uses for it that I can't list them all. Some of these uses were: split-rail fences, roofing shingles, tool handles, telegraph poles, railroad ties, and furniture. Its resistance to rot and decay made it a very popular wood indeed. The long-lasting nature of chestnut wood can still be seen by the firm, solid snags that remain in our forests today. And it was definitely one of the primary species that mountain people burned as firewood to keep their homes warm during the long, cold Winters.

It was truly one of the worst natural tragedies of our time when the chestnut blight destroyed nearly all of the native American chestnut trees. The blight, which is caused by a fungus, was first noticed in the New York Zoological Garden in 1904. It was accidentally introduced there on some plants that came from Asia. Within about 40 to 45 years almost all of the chestnut trees in this country were dead. And many of those trees were nearly 100 feet tall and three to five feet in diameter. There are reports of some trees which measured 13 to 15 feet in diameter!

Almost from the beginning of the blight's occurrence, scientists began searching for cures. Nothing was very successful. And to further complicate the problem, the blight found its way to Europe, where it devastated chestnut trees in Italy by the 1930's and France by the 1950's.

However, in recent years the blight seems to have cured itself in Italy. Noticing this, a French scientist began work to help speed up nature's healing process. It seems that the fungus eventually weakens to a point where the tree can defeat it. And when weak fungus and strong fungus come in contact, they both seem to weaken, allowing the tree to recover. The blight in Italy is almost gone now and France is curing it at a fast rate.

There are high hopes by scientists that this will happen in the United States in the future. The trick will be to get the weak strain of the fungus to spread naturally through our forests, just as the first fungus did over a half century ago. This occurred faster in Europe because many of the chestnut trees grew in pure stands and groves. However, in this country the chestnut was very widespread and grew in mixed stands with many other tree species, which complicates things. But scientists are optimistic that if they can help speed up the spreading process, nature will eventually take care of things. We'll just have to be patient and see how this works out.

There are two major research centers, one in Connecticut and one in West Virginia, which are working to solve the problem of the chestnut blight. Hopefully, within our lifetimes the beautiful and valuable American chestnut will once again take its rightful place in our mountain forests.

Ranger's Notebook – Chestnut blight kills the tree above ground, but does not affect the root system. The trees often re-sprout from these roots, making young chestnut seedlings and saplings common in our forests. However, by the time these small trees reach big enough size to bear nuts, the blight kills them back and the re-sprouting process begins once again.

July 13, 1979 –

The Appalachian Mountains – in my opinion the most beautiful and interesting stretch of land in this country – rise in southern Canada's provinces of Quebec and Newfoundland and traverse the entire eastern United States until they reach their end in South Carolina, Georgia, and Alabama.

By air, this distance is nearly 1,600 miles, but by road it is well over 2,000 miles. The mountains begin in Canada's Atlantic Time Zone, follow the Eastern Time Zone for most of their distance, and by the time they reach Alabama have crossed into the Central Time Zone.

In spite of the great length of the mountain chain, and though it covers two countries and several states, there are many similarities to be found in comparing any sections of the Appalachians. These similarities range from plants and animals to the people and their lifestyles.

Of course, many of the larger animals, such as white-tailed deer and black bears, are common throughout the entire Appalachian range. But what amazes me are instances where a certain species of lizard or some other small animal, or a small plant species, occurs on a mountain in the southern Appalachians and is found nowhere else except southern Canada.

One very interesting animal that demonstrates the strong ecological bond of the entire Appalachian system is the snow bunting. These beautiful white birds spend their summers in the Arctic. As the summer ends they migrate southward with many of them stopping in southern Quebec. There they find the two things they need in order to survive: food, often in the form of seeds from the three-toothed cinquefoil plant; and open areas where winter winds are strong enough to keep snow from completely covering their food supply.

When they go further south, they tend toward the beaches of the East coast where the strong winds keep the snow cover light. But there is one exception! Snow buntings have been observed in the southern mountains of North Carolina and Tennessee (Roan Mountain in particular), far inland and far south of their normal wintering grounds. Here they find their two keys to survival: open areas, such as southern mountain balds, with strong winds; and abundant food supplies. And the food supply in these southern mountain openings is none other than the three-toothed cinquefoil, the same plant that is so common in Quebec, where the mountains originate!

From Canada to Georgia, many things help tie the Appalachian Mountains into one life system – the plants, the animals, the lifestyles, and the rugged terrain. I'll never cease to find wonder and enjoyment in the Appalachian Mountains.

In future columns, I hope to discuss further some of the unique qualities that bind the Appalachians together.

Ranger's Notebook – The highest temperature recorded to date on Brasstown Bald was 84 degrees Fahrenheit, while the lowest was 27 degrees below zero.

July 19, 1979 –

The balds of the southern Appalachians are some of the most interesting areas that occur in our mountains. Balds have puzzled and intrigued botanists and nature lovers over the years.

Many of these grassy, treeless openings seem to have occurred naturally. Others were no doubt places that had been cleared off by the Indians and then maintained by fire or some other method. Some balds were created by early settlers and farmers for grazing their animals. Almost every bald, regardless of its origin, was used for grazing purposes by the early pioneers, thus helping to keep these areas in an open condition.

Open mountain areas are characteristic of the Appalachians from Canada to Georgia. In Canada and New England, many of the openings are above the tree line, which helps to explain their origin. But the open areas in the southern Appalachians (from Virginia to Georgia) are not above the tree line. The tree line is the altitude above which trees normally will not grow. This altitude line varies depending upon how far north or south you are in the country. In fact, the southern mountains are not high enough to approach the tree line. Also, many balds occur in gaps which connect the higher peaks. Trees grow both above and below these balds, which adds to their mystery.

Plants and animals common in Canada are found in southern Appalachian balds. These include animals such as warblers and salamanders, and plants such as spruces, balsams, and azaleas.

Certain balds that have been "protected" in the past several years are beginning to grow back to shrubs and trees. This likely means that those particular balds were indeed created by man – either Indians or early farmers. Other balds, however, seem to be maintaining their open, grassy qualities, which adds to the mystery of the southern balds.

Balds have been favorite places over the years for Indians, hunters, farmers, botanists, biologists, hikers, and sightseers. These unique openings help add to the enchantment of the Appalachian Mountains.

Ranger's Notebook – Nearly 100 balds are known to have occurred in the southern Appalachians. Familiar names in north Georgia are Brasstown Bald, Tickanetly Bald, Big Bald Mountain, Rabun Bald, Hightower Bald, and Little Bald.

July 26, 1979 –

Much of the information for this week's column was provided by Skip Stewart, who serves as the Camp Director of our residential YCC Camp, which is housed at Young Harris College. (See previous column written on June 27). This is Skip's third year of summer involvement with our program. For the past nine years, he has been a teacher in the Georgia school system. Skip has a Bachelor's degree in Biology and a Masters degree in Environmental Education, which makes him a perfect fit to direct our YCC Camp. Skip, his wife Brenda, and son Will live in Trion, Georgia.   - DK.

YCC Spike Camps -

One of our Camp Young Harris YCC work crews, named the "Purple Banded Geckos," has just completed a week of spike camp and they think the experience was well worth it. Normally we return to Young Harris College to eat and sleep each evening after a hard day's work somewhere out in the Chattahoochee National Forest. Spike camp is literally camping out somewhere in the forest near a work project, saving time and expense by not having to travel back and forth each day, and also giving the YCC'ers a camping experience.

This spike camp was at Lake Winfield Scott. It gave the group of seven campers and their Counselor/Supervisor a chance to get away from their normal routine of YCC life. The members of the Purple Banded Geckos were: Steve Manor of Savannah; Ted Bulick of Kennesaw; Joree Langley of Yatesville; Wade Crittenden of Austell; Stuart Bowen of Senoia; Jeff Sanders of Temple; Eric Granum, Youth Leader, of Tucker; and Dave Snow, Counselor, of Trion.

The work projects at Lake Winfield Scott included building a rock wall and steps at the beach area; picnic table construction; erosion control work; putting up sign markers on the Buffalo Nut Trail; and trail construction and maintenance.

The campers prepared their own meals and did some light maintenance work on their spike camp cabin. Meals included eggs, bacon, cereal, toast, and orange juice for breakfast; sandwiches and drinks for lunch; and hamburger steaks, spaghetti, hot dogs, pork chops, and vegetables for the dinner meals.

Environmental education activities took place in the evenings. One night there was a "nature snoop" or scavenger hunt session;

there were leaf collection and tree identification lessons; and plant grids to determine what kinds and how many small plants occur in a given forest area. Each camper kept a log book and they each wrote a poem about something they had discovered or learned during the week. At summer's end all log books and poems, as well as other information, will be compiled into a publication and each camper will receive a copy.

The campers had various thoughts about spike camp. "The cooking was a challenge for me, but it was great fun," said Langley, while Crittenden commented that "knowing you had to eat what you cooked made you more aware and cautious of food preparation."

Bulick said, "There's plenty of hard work involved. Planting grass seed, doing erosion control work, and trail maintenance around the lake and at Slaughter Creek Gap sure kept us busy. The work was tough, but I actually like it," said Bulick. Sanders added that "it's nice to know that our work will influence the environment in the right direction for years to come."

"A really neat thing about spike camp," explained counselor Snow, "is that these young men get to do things for themselves, learn about conservation, and respect nature."

"I get a great deal of enjoyment out of the environmental education activities," said Granum. "I especially like the ornithology and dendrology lessons;" while Manor said, "I like it all – the hard work, the backpacking, and recreation. I just like everything."

"Spike camp is definitely hard work," said Bowen, "But it's also good times. It's a great experience and will make a lasting impression on all of us. I would recommend this to anyone."

Ranger's Notebook – The Youth Conservation Corps (YCC) program continues to be very successful nationwide. There are camps run by state agencies, as well as the Forest Service in the U.S. Department of Agriculture, and various U.S. Department of Interior agencies. These latter agencies include the Fish & Wildlife Service, the National Park Service, and the Bureau of Land Management. Congress established and funded the YCC program beginning in 1970. It has been labeled a "work, learn, and earn" program.

Bertha and Joe Mummaw are spending their summer at the top of Georgia, living and working on Brasstown Bald, Georgia's highest mountain. The Mummaws are participants in the U.S. Forest Service Volunteer Program.

A retired electrician, Joe is the resident handyman at the U.S. Forest Service Visitor Information Center on Brasstown. He helps the staff with daily cleanup chores and takes care of interior maintenance needs. One of Joe's lifetime hobbies has been landscape architecture. He spends hours working on the grounds and flower beds adjacent to the buildings and parking lots. He works hard to make Brasstown Bald the showplace of north Georgia.

Bertha is a registered nurse. She has helped improve our first aid facilities at the Visitor Center and has occasionally needed to use her nursing skills to assist visitors. Both Joe and Bertha also assist our regular staff in greeting visitors and answering questions. They spend several hours each week in the evenings talking with visitors who come up the mountain after the center is closed for the day. The Mummaws keep in shape by hiking about four miles a day, picking up litter along the trails as they go.

Bertha and Joe first learned about the Forest Service Volunteer Program through a publication of the American Association of Retired Persons. In 1977 and 1978 they volunteered as Campground Hosts at Morganton Point Recreation Area, a Forest Service campground in Fannin County.

When asked why they do volunteer work, Bertha explained, "We have enjoyed good health and a good life and volunteer work is my way of showing my gratitude." Joe agreed and added, "I wanted to give something back to help the country and the environment."

The Mummaws are originally from Lancaster, Pennsylvania. Joe worked nine years with Pennsylvania Power and Light, and then for 32 years with RCA Corporation. Bertha was in charge of the school hospital at Franklin & Marshall College for eight years and then served as the nurse at Stephens Vocational Trade School.

When Joe retired, the winter sunshine lured them to Tamarac, Florida. There they are very active in the church, where they serve as deacon and deaconess, and also serve on the property committee. Joe is also an officer for their local clubhouse.

At Brasstown Bald Joe has had time to work on his newest hobby – wood carving. He already has carved a large pack of hound dogs and is now working on deer, ducks, and a cardinal. Bertha spends time baking and testing new recipes. The regular staff at the Visitor Center benefits from Bertha's hobby by eating her finished products.

Bertha and Joe's many varied talents and cheerful personalities have made them valuable members of the summer staff at Brasstown Bald Visitor Center.

<u>August 9, 1979</u> –

Today's column continues with historical sketches of forestry-related events that took place from 1861 to 1875.

1861-1870 – Iowa, Kansas, Dakota Territory, Nebraska, Minnesota, and Missouri passed laws encouraging the planting of forest trees.

1864 – "Man and Nature," the classic scientific work by George Perkins Marsh was published. This book sounded a warning about man's waste of the land and helped lead to the establishment of the U.S. Forest Reserves.

1867 – The Michigan and Wisconsin legislatures provided for inquiries into forest conditions and needs, and set up tree-growing bounties and tax exemptions.

1869 – A forestry committee was appointed under the State Board of Agriculture in Maine to develop a state forest policy.

1870 – The U.S. Census included a survey of forest resources for the first time.

1871 – A Federal Act provided $5,000 for "protection of timberlands." This was primarily intended for the protection of naval timber reservations. It was the first appropriation made directly for the protection of publicly owned timber in the United States. The next year, $10,000 was made available for the protection of public lands in general.

The great Peshtigo fire in Wisconsin was one of the worst in American history. Homes, towns, and settlements were swept away by the flames, while 1,500 people lost their lives and 1,280,000 acres were burned over.

1872 – Arbor Day was instituted in Nebraska on April 19 to stimulate tree planting in the prairie country. The observance of Arbor Day has since spread to every state and to many foreign countries.

Yellowstone National Park was reserved as a "pleasuring ground," the beginning of the National Park system.

A tree planting tax law in Maine provided for 20-year tax exemptions for land planted to trees.

A Wildland Commission was created in New York to consider state ownership of wild lands lying north of the Mohawk River.

1873 – Congress passed the first timber culture act, which granted a homesteader a patent to 160 acres of land in the Great Plains if he agreed to plant one-fourth of the land to trees. Later laws changed and finally eliminated the tree planting provision; but many early-day tree groves and shelterbelts were established by homesteaders under this act.

The American Association for the Advancement of Science held its annual meeting in Portland, Maine. Following an address by Dr. Franklin B. Hough, entitled, "On the Duty of Governments in the Preservation of Forests," a committee was appointed to urge Congress and state legislatures "to promote the cultivation of timber and the preservation of forests" and to recommend proper legislation for accomplishing this.

Lectures on forestry were started at Yale University, perhaps the earliest offered by an American university. Courses of instruction in forestry were begun the following year at Cornell University and in 1881 at the University of Michigan. By 1887 forestry instruction was also being given at the Agricultural Colleges in New Hampshire, Massachusetts, Michigan State, Missouri, and Iowa, as well as universities in Pennsylvania and North Carolina. It would not be until the late 1890's, however, that full professional forestry training, resulting in a college degree, was offered by an American university.

1875 – The American Forestry Association was organized on September 10 in Chicago. Its objectives were "the protection of the existing forests of the country, and the promotion of the propagation and planting of useful trees."

August 16, 1979 –

Information for today's column was provided by Debbie Day, who coordinates the youth programs, the senior citizen program, and the volunteer program for the Brasstown Ranger District.

This summer the Brasstown Ranger District has been blessed with three retired volunteers, whose tireless work has been invaluable to our programs. John Brooks has volunteered his time as the Campground Host at Lake Winfield Scott. Bob and Ruth Stager worked as volunteer house parents for the YCC Camp at Young Harris College, while also performing Campground Host duties at Lake Chatuge Campground.

John Brooks, known to everyone as "Pops," has been assisting campers and day-use visitors at Lake Winfield Scott for the past three summers. When asked why he keeps coming back, he simply replied, "I just love it. I've been coast to coast and I haven't found a spot as nice as Lake Winfield Scott." Pops said that many of the campers feel the same way. "The campers like the privacy afforded by the separation of the campsites, the hot showers, and most of all the quiet and solitude at Lake Winfield Scott."

Pops was born in Chicago. He worked for a railroad and then owned a retail shoe store for 20 years. In 1971 he moved to Houston, Texas to live with his son's family. What does he do when not participating in the Forest Service Volunteer Program? "I keep busy taking care of grandkids, while my son and daughter-in-law work," he said.

According to Pops the number of visitors to Lake Winfield Scott has picked up in the past few weeks. There has been an even mix of in-state and out-of-state campers, he said. Pops requests that any visitors needing information or assistance to please seek him out.

Bob and Ruth Stager traveled to the Brasstown Ranger District from Chipley, Florida. Bob retired as the owner-manager of a life insurance agency in 1975. Ruth retired in 1974 as a registered nurse. They own a van and tent camper and have enjoyed camping for many years. They also enjoy organic gardening, rug hooking, wood working, and various crafts.

After raising three children, the Stagers were well qualified for their volunteer job as house parents for our Young Harris YCC Camp. Both Stagers helped with the weekend and evening recreation activities for the teenagers. Bob was a big hit in the indoor recreation hall where he instructed and played pool with the campers – sometimes for hours on end during the rainy weather outside. Ruth's nurse training came in handy for many of the first aid situations that occurred during camp.

The Stagers also served as Campground Hosts at the Lake Chatuge Campground. They have been very active with litter pick up, and the appearance of the area definitely improved. They discussed litter control with the visitors and it all seems to have had a positive impact.

The Brasstown Ranger District was fortunate to have had great volunteers this summer in Pops Brooks and Ruth and Bob Stager.

August 23, 1979 –

We left off in our last historical forestry sketches with the year 1875. Many forestry historians feel like the real beginning of American forestry started in 1876, just 100 years after the Declaration of Independence, when Congress authorized the appointment of a special forestry agent. Over the next 25 years, the "forestry movement," as it was called at the time, primarily entailed a campaign of public education. Large scale thefts and exploitation of timber resources were common and the government began to move toward a forest policy for federally owned timberlands.

It's kind of amazing to realize that professional, scientific forest management in the United States began to form only about 100 years ago.

1876 – A special agent, Dr. Franklin B. Hough, a physician, statistician, and naturalist of Lowville, New York, was appointed by Fredrick Watts, the U.S. Commissioner of Agriculture, to: 1) gather data on the supply and demand for timber and other forest products for the present and future; 2) to report on means successfully used abroad to manage forests; 3) to identify means that might be used in the country to preserve and renew forests; and 4) to investigate the influence of forests on climate.

A bill was introduced in Congress to ensure preservation of forests of the public domain adjacent to the sources of navigable rivers and other streams.

1877 – Congress granted its first appropriation, $6,000, to obtain natural resource information prior to establishing a Division of Forestry in the U.S. Department of Agriculture.

Carl Schurz, a German immigrant, statesman and student of forestry, who became Secretary of the Interior in 1877, was among the first to propose and urge the establishment of federal forest reservations, as well as the scientific handling of the forests. In his native

Germany, forests were managed so that there was always a supply of wood. Trees were regularly cut and then replaced. Schurz believed the same could be done in his adopted country.

Secretary Schurz and J.A. Williamson, a fiery advocate of public forest control who had just become Commissioner of the General Land Office, completely reorganized the system of protecting and caring for public timberlands. District land registers and receivers were relieved of their timberland protection responsibilities. A force of specially trained timber agents was organized and a drive was started against timber thievery and exploitation of public lands. A new circular of instructions for the timber agents was issued.

Connecticut set up a forest inquiry commission.

1877 – 1883 – Three comprehensive reports were prepared by Dr. Hough and submitted to Congress.

August 30, 1979 –

Continuing with the early history of federal forestry work, we find Congress becoming more and more interested in regulating and managing our nation's forest reserves.

1878 – The Free Timber Act and The Timber and Stone Act were passed by Congress. Until that time there had been no distinction between timberlands and other lands, and also no honest way to acquire public timberlands. The Free Timber Act gave the people of nine western states the right to cut timber at will on mineral lands for both domestic and mining purposes. The Timber and Stone Act authorized the sale of public lands that were valuable for timber production, but not fit for agriculture, if they had not been previously offered for sale. The minimum price was $2.50 per acre and the maximum area that could be sold to one person, association, or corporation was 160 acres. The "law of unintended consequences" kicked in, however. The provisions of these two laws proved to be impractical and unenforceable and it opened the door to widespread fraud, wholesale timber cutting, and destruction of many forest areas. For example, in 1885 the government sought to recover the value of 60 million board feet of high grade lumber stolen from public forests by a single California company.

A bill was introduced in Congress, based upon the ideas of Schurz and Williamson, providing for the disposition and management of public timber and timberlands. All public lands bearing timber of commercial value would be withdrawn from sale or other disposal. Lands valuable chiefly for timber would be held by the government to prevent waste and destruction by fire. The bill called for continuous restoration and reproduction of the forests, with only a gradual sale of trees that were most valuable as timber.

An office of Forester would be established in the Department of Interior. The President could appoint as many Foresters at $2,500 per year as he deemed necessary for the proper care, custody, preservation, and appraisement of the timber on public lands. Fines of up to $1,000 and one year in prison, plus double the amount of damage caused, would be set for anyone convicted of willingly or negligently setting fire to any woods, prairie, or ground on public lands; or anyone who permitted a fire to pass from his property to that of another.

The bill failed to pass Congress!

The first state game commissions were established in New Hampshire and California.

1879 – Congress created a Public Lands Commission to codify public land laws and to recommend wise disposal and/or management of these lands. The Commission proposed a law to correct abuses on valuable timber lands and to set aside portions of these lands as forest reserves. The Commission's report to Congress in 1880 contributed greatly to the Forest Reserve Act that finally passed in 1891.

1881 – The forest agency of the Department of Agriculture was made the formal Division of Forestry. It had no forest lands under its control. It served only to establish facts about forests and forestry. An agent was sent to Europe to study forestry there. In 1884 the duty of setting up experiments with timber was added to the responsibilities of the new Division.

1882 – An American Forestry Congress was organized in Cincinnati, Ohio and Bernhard E. Fernow was selected as its first Secretary.

1884 – The Senate Standing Committee on Agriculture became the Committee on Agriculture and Forestry.

September 7, 1979 –

One last historical column today. Then I'll hold off for a few weeks. I have, however, received several comments from readers who

said they enjoy these historical sketches.
Today will bring us up to 1890 and the verge
of when the National Forests were established
in 1891. As we have seen, interest in forestry
and getting the management of forests under
some sort of control and professional,
scientific management had been gathering
steam and support for the previous 25 years
or so. But there were many stops and starts,
impediments, and dead ends encountered
before there was finally enough momentum to
turn things around. The era of forest
exploitation, widespread timber theft, and
abuse of forest lands was coming to an end.
And none too soon.

1885 – New York was the first state to undertake public forest administration. It created the huge Adirondack State Forest Reserve and set up a State Forest Commission, which has continued in operation uninterrupted since then. A comprehensive fire control law was also passed.

Six bills were introduced in Congress for creation of federal forest reserves. None passed.

California created a State Board of Forestry. Colorado and Ohio took similar action later in the year.

1886 – The Division of Forestry was given permanent statutory rank in the U.S. Department of Agriculture under Dr. Bernhard E. Fernow. He was a Prussian expert on forestry and the first formal Chief of the Division.

1887 – The Division of Forestry issued a "Report on the Relation of Railroads to Forest Supplies and Forestry." It estimated the vast amount of timber used in building and maintaining the railroads, and it warned against exhaustion of our bountiful timber resource from wasteful cutting.

Pennsylvania set up a Forest Inquiry Commission.

1888 – An Irrigation Division of the U.S. Geological Survey was established and the Secretary of Interior was given authority to regulate forest areas around reservoir sites and areas where irrigation was necessary.

Another comprehensive bill was introduced in Congress for the protection and administration of forests in the public domain. It provided for a Commissioner of Forests who would sub-divide forest reserves into divisions and districts; organize a "forest service;" appoint forest inspectors or forest rangers; "establish a practical system of forestry;" and make reasonable rules and regulations for the prevention of trespass, the control of forest fires, and the "conservation of the forest growth." This bill also failed to pass, but was another important step toward sound and progressive forestry legislation. This bill was drafted by Bernhard Fernow.

A law was enacted forbidding timber trespass on Indian reservations.

1889 – A law passed regulating the sale and use of dead timber on Indian lands, an important development in American Forestry.

The American Forestry Congress presented a resume of timber trespass and timber thievery on public lands to President Benjamin Harrison. The report showed that between 1881 and 1887 over $36 million worth of timber was unlawfully taken from public lands and that only about $475,000 was recovered by the government. A former Federal Inspector prepared the report.

September 11, 1979 –

Writing these weekly columns can become a chore, with all of my other duties as Assistant Ranger on the Brasstown District. I have responsibility for managing the fire, recreation, special uses, visitor center, law enforcement, and the youth, senior citizen, and volunteer programs. Of course, I also supervise several employees, monitor my budget, purchase supplies, and have other office duties, too.

And recently, I've become a member of the Forest Planning Team. That duty requires frequent trips to our Supervisor's Office in Gainesville for meetings, attending training sessions, and providing input on certain portions of our draft Forest Plan. Later, I will provide more information about the Forest Plan and what it all means to you. But even though I'm pretty busy, communicating with the public through these weekly columns is well worth it. My supervisor, District Ranger Jack McCormick, supports this effort and certainly the local public in Towns and Union counties has provided me with lots of positive feedback on the columns.

I'm truly lucky to have several employees to help me with my programs. Odell Ballew handles our building and utility maintenance at campgrounds and at Brasstown Bald, as well as various other duties. Debbie Day coordinates all of the human resource programs. Lindsay Gregory and Jessie King work in recreation, visitor information, and law enforcement. And we *also have a fine staff handling various office duties.*

A recent addition to my staff, and really to the entire District staff, has been Frances Mason, who had formerly been the Assistant Ranger over at Dahlonega. She had been traveling there each day from Blairsville, where she and husband Charles live. Charles Mason is one of our Forestry Technicians here on the Brasstown District. So now Frances has a much shorter commute and we have another very capable and valuable employee. With Frances' experience, I don't have to worry about certain things. She is a tremendous help in all aspects of recreation and she has taken on the day to day planning and management of activities at Brasstown Bald Visitor Center.

And one other benefit is that Frances has volunteered to write occasional columns for me when I get busy. Debbie Day has done that in the past, too. Frances wrote today's column and she plans to do next week's column, also. I can't thank her enough and I think you will enjoy reading what she writes.

With the students back in school and the coming of cool weather, visitation at Forest Service recreation areas has dropped off noticeably. That happens every year after Labor

Day. Let's look back and see what kind of season we had.

This past Summer we had gas shortages, the truckers strike, and cool, rainy weather. All these things affected our recreation use. Comparing campground fees collected between this year and last year, recreation use was down 18 percent at Lake Chatuge and down 13 percent at Lake Winfield Scott. Camping use was actually down by as much as 40 percent for short periods of time.

At Brasstown Bald Visitor Center, the summer weather was generally cold, windy, and rainy. It affected our visitor use, too. June visitation was down 17 percent from last year, while July was down by 35 percent.

These visitor figures had a negative effect, too, on tourism dollars for local businesses. Gas stations, stores, restaurants, and marinas all suffered this summer. Despite the overall low numbers for the summer, thankfully August at least had a five percent visitor increase over last year, which lessened the overall impact.

September is traditionally a slow recreation time in north Georgia before the heavy use "color season" in October and early November. We're now busy preparing for that and we expect a great Fall!

September 21, 1979 –

Today's column is written by Frances Mason, District Recreation Specialist. Frances is a Florida native and has a Forestry Degree from the University of Florida.

If you've never been to Brasstown Bald in October, you don't know what you're missing! The view from the top of the mountain is excellent during any season, but especially lovely in the Fall.

The cool, crisp air clears out the summer mists allowing visibilities of up to 100 miles. On a very clear day Stone Mountain and the Atlanta skyline are visible to the south. Clingman's Dome, Tennessee is visible 60 miles to the north on most Fall days. Since North Carolina is so close, many mountain peaks are visible there, but you can also see into South Carolina to the east.

Other prominent landmarks to see are Georgia's second and third highest mountains, Rabun Bald and High Tower Bald. The rocky Yonah Mountain and Currahee Mountain stand as lonely sentinels above the flatter land southwest of Clarksville. Lake Chatuge takes on

113

a new look from Brasstown, the blue water and red clay shorelines resembling a giant, oddly shaped jewel.

These views are only half the show, however. Mid-October brings out brilliant and colorful fall foliage. Fiery reds, blazing yellows, purples, deep oranges, and bronzes mix with patches of green pine needles to present a breathtaking scene.

Literally thousands of people travel to Brasstown Bald every October to view the autumn colors. Sundays are usually the busiest days. The one-day attendance record of 6,044 was set on a Sunday in 1970. Saturday crowds are large, too, often bringing over 2,000 visitors. Weekdays average about 350 visitors each day. Last year, almost 25,000 people visited Brasstown Bald in October.

These visitors are all guests of the U.S. Forest Service and most of them stop in at our Visitor Center. The facility offers an exhibit hall containing exhibits on the theme of "Man and the Mountain," and a 15-minute slide presentation is shown every 30 minutes in the Mountain Top Theater. Of course, the observation deck with its panoramic views of the Fall colors seems to be the most popular spot in October. Forest Service personnel are on duty there to point out landmarks and to answer questions.

Other facilities include a 350-car parking lot, a picnic area, restrooms, and a concession building with soft drink and food machines. A concessionaire operated bus shuttle takes visitors from the parking lot to the top of the mountain for a small fee. Or visitors can walk the half-mile distance via a hiking trail for free.

Late September is already bringing out the purples and reds of the sourwood and dogwood trees. It won't be much longer before Brasstown Bald Mountain leads Georgia into the Fall color season. Make your plans now to come visit us and see the beautiful colors from Brasstown Bald.

September 26, 1979 –

In our Eastern mountains we usually don't have Fall forest fires until October or November, but out West the dry weather can cause fire conditions to occur in mid to late summer. So, we normally send firefighters to help with emergencies in the Western states. This gives our crews more experience and training to handle our fires when they occur later in the Fall, in addition to providing much needed assistance to our Western firefighters.

In early August, Brasstown District Ranger Jack McCormick led a 20-man firefighting crew from the Chattahoochee National Forest, which flew from Atlanta to Spokane, Washington. From there they took a bus 150 miles to northern Idaho where they helped battle the Templeton Lake Fire for three days.

After that, the crew was sent to the Interagency Fire Center in Boise, Idaho to rest and re-group before going to the Mortar Creek Fire on the Challis National Forest in east-central Idaho. They helped fight that forest fire for a week.

The Mortar Creek Fire was the big one in the Idaho Primitive Area that we all saw featured on numerous TV newscasts for several days. Before being brought under control, this fire burned over 60,000 acres. Jack said this fire was particularly tiring for the crews to fight because the country there was so steep and rough. Since the fire was burning in a "primitive area," the work was all done by hand (no power tools or vehicles were allowed) and they had to walk in and out 5 to 10 miles per day. Several hundred firefighters were required in order to control this fire.

Jack's crew then returned to Atlanta by charter plane from Boise, Idaho, thinking that their firefighting was over for the summer. This was far from true, however.

On September 16 and September 18 we sent out a total of 14 more firefighters from the Chattahoochee National Forest to help deal with an emergency in California. Seven of our personnel flew from Knoxville, Tennessee to Los Angeles, where they were put to work on the Sage Fire on the Angeles National Forest. This fire, which burned in chaparral, manzanita, brush, and scattered Coulter pine and sugar pine, eventually burned over 35,000 acres, including several homes. It took over 2,000 firefighters from all over the country to control the blaze. The weather there was hot and dry. The smoke from the fire added to southern California's air pollution problem, which was already classified as extremely dangerous to health. The firefighters had to wear damp face masks in order to be able to breathe.

Seven more Georgia firefighters flew out from Atlanta to Sacramento, California and ended up on the Chili Bar Fire on the El Dorado National Forest near Placerville, California. These firefighters were in big timber country, a far cry from the brush of southern

California. The trees were mostly Douglas fir, sugar pine, Jeffrey pine, and western red cedar. The crew worked in several capacities, including fire suppression, mop-up, and night patrol.

All of our District personnel returned last week, extremely tired and happy to be home. The experience gained out West this summer will be very useful when fire season comes to the Chattahoochee National Forest in a couple of months.

Forest Service employees from the Brasstown Ranger District, who assisted with the western firefighting efforts this summer included: Danny Owenby, Zane Rogers, Jack McCormick, Charles Hughes, Jerry Gilreath, Ronnie Kelley, Lindsay Gregory, Milton Bradley, Vic Payne, Martin Kindred, Debbie Day, J.B. King, Jesse Payne, Pete Mauldin, Bryan Souther, David Collins, and Grady Groves.

October 4, 1979 –

Today's column is written by Frances Mason, Recreation Forester on the Brasstown Ranger District of the Chattahoochee National Forest.

Now that the trees are starting to display their Fall wardrobes, many people have asked, "What makes the leaves change colors?" In order to explain that, I first need to tell you what makes leaves green.

A leaf is green because of the presence of a group of pigments known as chlorophylls. When chlorophylls are abundant in a leaf's cells, as occurs during the growing season, the greens dominate and mask out the colors of any other pigments that are present.

Chlorophyll's vital function is to capture the sun's energy and use it to produce the tree's food – simple sugars from water and carbon dioxide. In this food manufacturing process, chlorophyll is constantly being used up. But during the growing season it is replaced rapidly, the supply remains high, and the leaves stay green.

When Autumn approaches, influences both inside and outside the tree cause chlorophyll to be replaced more slowly. Thus, the "masking effect" of green slowly diminishes and other pigments that have been present all along begin to show through. These other pigments are called carotenoids. Their brilliant yellows and oranges tint the leaves of such hardwood tree species as hickories, ash, maple, yellow poplar, black cherry, and sassafras.

The reds and purples and their blended combinations that decorate Fall foliage come from another group of pigments called anthocyanins. These pigments are not present in the leaf during the growing season like the carotenoids. Instead, they develop in late summer as the result of complex chemical interactions in the leaf. The brighter the sunlight during this period, the greater the production of anthocyanins and the more brilliant the resulting color display. The sharpest colors occur when the days are bright and cool and the nights are chilly, but not freezing.

In our forests the anthocyanins show up most vividly in maples, oaks, sourwood, sweetgum, dogwood, and persimmon. When these pigments combine with the carotenoids, we see deeper oranges, fiery reds, and bronze colors.

It may be good to know that leaves change colors because of complex chemical interactions and weather influences, but personally I like to daydream about Mother Nature walking through the forest dressing up her trees in new Fall outfits. Naturally, she would give the prettiest suits to her favorite trees. My personal favorites are the maples whose leaves are a peachy, orange color.

Or maybe you picture Jack Frost as the one who does all the work. He sneaks in at night with buckets and buckets of paint to create the splendid tapestry of colors that October is so famous for.

Whatever your personal fantasy about how the leaves change color, there is no denying the beauty of it all. The Chattahoochee National Forest offers thousands of acres in which you can enjoy this magnificent color display.

October 10, 1979 –

Fire season is officially open now, so I want to remind everyone to be careful with any brush burning or hunting camp fires. Although we've had a lot of rain lately, it's always a good idea to respect fire and not take any unnecessary chances with it.

With deer hunting season opening three weeks earlier than normal this year, there will be many hunters in the woods during peak fire season. You'll need to be very careful with camp fires, matches, cigarettes, and so forth.

Woodsy the Owl was a hit at the Sorghum Festival Parade in Blairsville last Saturday. Even though Smokey Bear is still the Forest Service's most popular symbol, Woodsy is fast becoming a favorite with the kids. Many school groups are now planning litter pick-up days and other activities centered on the Woodsy Owl theme of "Give a hoot; don't pollute." Get in touch with us here at the office for more information about Woodsy Owl and how we can help you with activities around the anti-littering theme.

We now have two films at our office that will be of interest to school groups and other organizations – "Smokey Bear;" and "Help Woodsy Spread the Word." If your group would like us to present a program, please call us to schedule something – 745-6928.

October 18, 1979 –

Today's historical snippets run from 1890 through 1893 and include the 1891 law that created the National Forest System.

1890 – The cutting of 20 million board feet of green timber annually on the Menominee Indian Reservation in Wisconsin was authorized by an act of Congress. This was the first federal law regulating the cutting of live timber on government-managed lands.

Sequoia, Yosemite, and General Grant National Parks were created, all in the Sierra Mountains of California. Total area at first was 838,770 acres; eventually this was nearly doubled by the addition of lands from adjacent forest reserves and national forests. The General Grant Park was later changed to be called Kings Canyon National Park, which was finally combined with Sequoia National Park.

1891 – By an Act of Congress, approved March 3, 1891, the President was given power to establish forest reserves from the public domain (26 Stat. 1103). This was the beginning of the National Forest System. The provision was attached as a rider to a bill revising the federal land laws.

On March 30, President Harrison created the first reserve – the Yellowstone Timberland Reserve, an area of 1,239,040 acres in Wyoming. Today, these lands are part of the Shoshone and Teton National Forests.

On October 16, President Harrison signed a proclamation withdrawing 1,198,080 acres in Colorado known as the White River Plateau Timberland Reserve, now known as the White River National Forest.

Before his term had expired, President Harrison had set aside forest reservations totaling over 13 million acres. No plan of operation or management was passed by Congress, so the reserves were simply "closed" areas.

North Carolina set up a Forest Inquiry Commission.

Maine authorized its State Land Agent to serve also as State Forest Commissioner with the duty to collect data on forest fire losses, forest waste, and the effects of forest area reduction on watersheds.

1892 – President Harrison proclaimed eight more Timberland Reserves – Pike's Peak, Plum Creek, South Platte, and Battlement Mesa, all in Colorado; Pecos River in New Mexico; Bull Run in Oregon; San Gabriel in California; and Afognak in Alaska.

Gifford Pinchot was employed as the first professional Forester in the United States, working at the Biltmore Estate of George W. Vanderbilt in the mountains of western North Carolina.

1893 – New Hampshire set up a State Forestry Commission with responsibility for forestry education, as well as authority to purchase land for public purposes.

Five more timberland reserves were set aside by President Harrison: Sierra, San Bernardino, and Trabuco Canyon in California; Pacific in Washington, and Grand Canyon in Arizona, for a total of nearly 13.5 million acres during his administration. The next President, Grover Cleveland, added the Cascade Range and the Ashland Timberland Reserves in Oregon, which totaled over 4.5 million acres.

October 25, 1979 –

Debbie Day manages our human resource programs, including the Young Adult Conservation Corps. She contributes today's column.

Have you ever seen a yak in our north Georgia mountains? Well, contrary to popular belief, the Forest Service now has 10 of them working on the Brasstown Ranger District. Although not of the long-haired, four-footed variety these 11 young people are members of our Young Adult Conservation Corps (YACC) and are commonly referred to as YACC's, "yaks."

The purpose of the YACC program is to provide manpower for needed conservation projects on public lands, while also reducing unemployment among our young adults, 16 to 23 years of age. We have had the program for almost two years now and we are very pleased with the results.

District Ranger, Jack McCormick, puts it this way. "The YACC program is of benefit to the Forest Service and the youths, and therefore to the local community," said McCormick. "All YACCs must rotate out at the end of a year, which allows more young people to join the program and gain job skills and experience, which will help them to find a better job. In two years we have employed 36 local young adults," McCormick added. "The program benefits the Forest Service by allowing us to accomplish work that otherwise would remain undone."

Hard work is the name of the game for the YACC crew. The reward for their efforts goes far beyond the minimum wages they earn. Corps member Randy McClure says, "I chose this job because it's a good place to get started. If you get a good name for yourself here, you will have a good chance for jobs once this is finished." Most of the enrollees stated that the variety of the work, the new skills learned, and getting to work outdoors were big benefits of the program.

Joe Burnette is our YACC program's Work Supervisor, who leads the enrollees in a wide variety of projects. Currently, they are building a three-bay pole shed for hay storage at our Work Center. The YACCs cleared the land, had the trees sawed into lumber, and are well on their way to a finished product that they all can be proud of.

Other projects planned are: tree pruning, road maintenance, landscaping at Brasstown Bald, wildlife habitat improvement, assisting with landline surveying, and renovation projects at Lake Winfield Scott Campground.

Working on our outdoor projects are YACC enrollees: Randy McClure, Troy Dyer, Tim Hooper, Raymond King, Terry Davis, Jeff Hamlin, Eddie Dyer, and Jackie Abercrombie.

In addition to the outdoor projects, YACC enrollees Joy Gregory and Patsy Hughes are working in our office, learning useful skills and helping us to provide better service to the public.

YACC – a good investment in the present and for the future!

November 1, 1979 –

Our Brasstown Ranger District of the Chattahoochee National Forest includes land in both Towns and Union counties, two of the most scenic and beautiful counties in the entire southern Appalachians.

Many famous people and well known events have come from or taken place in these two counties, including athletic teams, politicians, civic organizations, schools, fairs and festivals, and more. But I'm willing to bet that most people are unaware of several of our "resident" champions. I'm referring to the several state and national champion trees that are located nearby.

There are 12 state champion trees located on the Brasstown District, six in each county. One of these is also a national champion. The Georgia Forestry Commission ranks champion trees using a formula based upon circumference, total height, and crown spread. Following are the champion trees and the counties in which they are located:

1) <u>Sweet (Black) Birch</u> – Union County
2) <u>Yellow Birch</u> – Towns County
3) <u>Pin Cherry</u> – Towns County

4) <u>Painted Buckeye</u> – Union County, and this tree is also currently a national champion
5) <u>Black Cherry</u> – Union County
6) <u>Black Locust</u> – Towns County
7) <u>Striped Maple</u> – Towns County
8) <u>Chestnut Oak</u> – Union County
9) <u>Northern Red Oak</u> – Union County
10) <u>Pitch Pine</u> – Towns County
11) <u>Virginia Pine</u> – Towns County
12) <u>Yellow Poplar</u> – Union County

This last tree has not been officially crowned yet, but it will be soon. It was just discovered about two weeks ago by Doug Gray, Assistant Ranger on the Brasstown Ranger District. The tree is located in the Jack's Gap area and measured 18-feet, 3-inches in circumference; 153 feet in total height; and had a crown spread of 89-feet, 6-inches. This tree is probably 200 to 300 years old, Doug said.

Of course, I'm sure you understand why we cannot give you the exact location for any of the 12 trees.

Employee Spotlight – Doug Gray's primary responsibilities are in managing our timber and wildlife programs, as well as supervising our land line surveying program. He has a

Forestry Degree from Auburn University in Alabama.

He says that finding a state champion yellow poplar tree was exciting for him. He now joins L.A. Rich, Charles Mason, Betty Taylor, and Frances Mason as employees from our District who have found a state champion tree.

Doug and his wife Janice, along with two children, Pam and Phil, have lived in Blairsville for three years. Previous job locations with the Forest Service for Doug have been in Alabama, Mississippi, and Florida, as well as Chatsworth, Georgia.

November 9, 1979 –

The increased emphasis on energy conservation, coupled with rapidly rising heating costs, has forced most Americans to make changes in their homes and/or their heating systems. Just a few short years ago it was uncommon for anyone to spend money improving the heating efficiency of their homes. Fuel oil, gas, electricity, propane, etc. were fairly cheap, so it didn't make good economic sense to spend several hundred or a thousand dollars just to save a few dollars here and there on heating bills. And very few people were genuinely concerned about saving energy.

How quickly things have changed! The days of cheap heat and energy unawareness are gone forever. Now, almost everyone is adding insulation to their attics and walls, lowering their thermostats, installing storm windows, and caulking or weather stripping around every crack and crevice.

Perhaps the most significant change that has occurred recently is the large number of homes that are being heated with wood. The increase in firewood demand has had quite an impact on National Forest management. We try to have enough free firewood (home use only) available in the forest for Union and Towns County residents. However, it's becoming more and more difficult to do so. In 1973 we issued only 84 firewood permits the entire Fall and Winter. This year we have already issued over 1200 permits. With this many people wanting firewood, it has been difficult to meet the demand.

Still, we realize the importance of the firewood program to the public. The Chattahoochee National Forest is currently studying the problem and will be trying hard to come up with new ways to meet future demand. We will keep you posted on any developments.

Here are a few reminders for those people who currently have one of our firewood permits:

1) Remember! The wood is for personal, home use only. It cannot be sold or traded for other goods.
2) There is a 10 cord limit. Don't get more than your share; leave some wood for others.
3) Stay within the designated areas. The boundaries are clearly marked.
4) If you're cutting any standing trees, make sure the stumps you leave are less than 12 inches high.
5) Failure to follow the regulations specified on the permit will result in losing your permit and paying a fine.
6) There is a lot of firewood available, but some of it is easier to get to than others. The easy wood, of course, goes fast, but with a little effort you should be able to get what you need.

In the future we hope we can come up with new ways to meet the ever increasing demand for firewood.

<u>__November 14, 1979 –__</u>

<u>WOOD BURNING FACTS AND HINTS</u>

  * A fireplace adds a certain charm to a room or den. It is also adequate for getting rid of early morning or evening chills in the Spring or Fall, but not so much in the Winter. And a fireplace can be a real lifesaver if your electricity is off for several days during a Winter ice storm. But all things considered, a fireplace is not an effective or efficient means of heating your home (or even a single room).

  During the cold Winter months, not even the most elaborate fireplaces will help you heat your home. In fact, you'll very likely have a net loss of heat. The primary reason for this is that a fireplace draws large quantities of warm air from your home and this warm air is lost out the chimney. It is replaced by cool outside air.

  For heat efficiency, modern wood burning stoves are best since they have draft controls that draw much smaller quantities of air than a fireplace. These metal stoves also retain heat for long periods of time and this heat radiates back into your home.

  * Last year more than 7.3 million green tons of free firewood were gathered from

National Forest lands across the country. This compared to only 1.1 million tons in 1973.

* Federal experts estimate that there is a minimum of 500 million dry tons of residue wood in public forests, private woodlands, and city clearing sites that could be turned into wood heat.

* Wood now makes up about two percent of our nation's fuel supply. Experts figure this could easily be increased to seven percent, which would save more than 2.5 million barrels of oil a day.

*Firewood should be dried a minimum of three months before burning and six months of drying would be even better. The drier your wood the more heat it gives off and the less creosote buildup you get in your chimney. Many people prefer using a lot of green wood because it lasts longer in the stove than dry wood. However, it does not give off more heat. Here's why. Green wood contains a high percentage of water, resins, and oils. It takes much of the heat from your fire just to evaporate this moisture from the wood so that it will burn. This results in a cooler fire. And cooler fires always mean a quicker creosote buildup in your chimney.

* Your chimney should be cleaned at least a couple of times a year to prevent

creosote buildup. If constructing a new chimney, make sure it rises above the roof line to get a good draw and prevent downdrafts. Downdrafts can also cause more than normal creosote formation. A chimney cap, open on four sides with the top closed, will help prevent downdrafts.

- continued next week -

November 22, 1979 –

MORE WOOD BURNING HINTS AND FACTS

* The fuel value of wood varies, depending upon species, density, and moisture content. While any wood will burn, the denser hardwoods make the best fuel because they burn slower and give off more heat per unit of volume than the lighter woods.

* Actually, a ton of air-dry wood of any species contains about the same amount of heat potential. The problem is that because of differences in density, it takes much more wood of certain species than others to weigh a ton. For instance, think how many more sticks of yellow-poplar it would take to weigh a ton than it would white oak or hickory. But a ton of either species, dried to the same level, should provide about the same amount of heat.

*Air drying wood for about six months will reduce its moisture content to approximately 20 percent. This is about as dry as you can get most woods without going to artificial means, such as oven drying.

* When air dried, 5,000 pounds of freshly cut white oak will weigh only 4,000 pounds. This means 1,000 pounds of moisture is gone from the wood that won't have to be evaporated off by your stove during burning, if only you'll let your wood dry for about six months. I know this isn't always possible, but it's sure worth it if you can.

* Remember – burning green wood means: a cooler fire and more creosote buildup in your chimney.

* An air dry cord of white pine weighs only about half as much as an air dry cord of oak or hickory.

* In the early 1800's in the Appalachian Mountains, it often took up to 20 or 25 cords of wood per year to heat a home using the fireplace. And even then, much of the house was very cool. Today's modern mountain home, with insulation, better construction, and more efficient wood stoves, can be heated using only about 4 to 6 cords in the same size house. Some things about the "good ol' days" weren't so good after all.

November 27, 1979 –

* Remembering from last week's article that the denser the wood the greater the heat output, here are the relative heat values for some of our most common wood species:

White ash -	High
Hickory -	Very High
Sugar maple -	High
Red maple -	Medium
Gum -	Medium
Mixed oaks -	High
Yellow poplar -	Low
Aspen -	Low
White pine -	Low
Shortleaf pine -	Medium
Dogwood -	Very High
Sassafras -	Low

* Different wood types leave different amounts of ash after burning. The ash residue of most woods will vary from 0.1 to 3.0 percent. Ash content can vary according to age, the part of the tree the wood comes from, and how much bark is left on the wood.

* Either steel plate or cast iron are good materials for wood stoves, though both materials have positive and negative aspects. Both materials are good for heat retention. Steel can warp, but this won't normally affect the functioning of the stove. Cast iron can crack, but this doesn't happen very often. Both materials can rust or eventually burn out. In general, the thicker the material, the longer it will last.

* You can ruin your stove, stovepipe, and chimney by burning very much trash, especially plastics. Many plastics contain chlorine and fluorine, which form very corrosive acids in a fire. Stovepipe can corrode clear through in just a year under such conditions.

* Though steel can warp, cast iron can crack, and either one can corrode, using firebrick or other liners will lessen these effects. This lining will keep the main stove body from getting too hot and the linings are easily replaced.

* It's a good idea for everyone to have a smoke alarm or two in their homes. The newer models are very dependable and can last for a year on just one battery. A wood caused fire will give off smoke that can easily be detected by a smoke alarm, thus setting off the buzzer.

These devices have saved thousands of lives in the past several years.

December 7, 1979 –

As mentioned in previous columns, our District is employing several local young people for one year as part of the Young Adult Conservation Corps (YACC) program. This program involves a lot of hard work, but also quite a bit of training, which will help prepare them for future employment.

Last Wednesday, seven of our YACC workers attended a chainsaw training session put on by J.B. King, who is one of our long-time Forest Service employees here on the Brasstown Ranger District. The session stressed the safety aspects of tree felling, limbing, bucking, and chainsaw maintenance. Each person had to pass both a written test and a field test in order to qualify as a government chainsaw operator. In addition, each new operator will spend several days working with an experienced man in the field. The training and experience gained here should serve these young people for many years to come.

On another note, the Arkaqua Trail has recently been designated a National Recreation

Trail. Extending for 5 ½ miles from the Brasstown Bald parking lot to Track Rock Gap, the Arkaqua Trail is considered one of the most interesting and beautiful trails in north Georgia. The trail drops a total of 2,500 feet, which means the wise hiker will begin at Brasstown Bald and hike downhill to Track Rock Gap. If you hike it in the other direction, you'd better be in good physical condition.

Many of the trees and plants that occur along the trail are not common this far south, which adds to the pleasure of the hike. The hike can be an enjoyable half-day trip. One word of caution though. There are some steep places in the middle and also several rock bluffs and cliffs within a few hundred feet of the trail. If you wander off the trail be very careful.

The Arkaqua Trail will provide a pleasurable hiking experience for many people for years to come.

December 13, 1979 –

Fall is just about gone now. Actually, the last three or four weeks have been signaling the start of Winter and the end of Fall. The change is usually gradual and doesn't catch us totally by surprise.

Most of us would agree that we're very lucky to be living where we can enjoy the distinctiveness of each of the four seasons. California, Arizona, and Florida are all nice places, but without the true change of seasons, something just doesn't seem right. I spent a year living in Arizona while in the Air Force and it was indeed a beautiful place with lots of interesting sights to see; but I sure did miss the Fall and Winter.

In the mid to southern Appalachians, our Winters aren't normally so severe that we can't enjoy them. The Winters here are nothing like those in Minnesota, Montana, or Maine; and in Minnesota you have such a short Summer and Fall that they're gone before you realize it. I should know because we lived in Minnesota, where I worked on the Superior National Forest, right before my transfer to Georgia. Having grown up in West Virginia, I much prefer this. In north Georgia the four seasons are just about equally balanced.

The Appalachian Mountain area is also perhaps the most beautiful section of our country in terms of diversity of plant life and physical features. The Rocky Mountains have their awesome and majestic splendor, but they sure don't have the variety of colors in the Fall like the Appalachians do. And some of the

Midwestern states that do have the nice Fall colors certainly don't have the mountains and other physical features that we have in the Appalachians. Here we have the best of both.

There are lots of things to be thankful for during the Holiday Season, not the least of which is the beauty of the area in which we live.

Our District has enjoyed a very fine work year and we've accomplished quite a bit, both in terms of resource management and service to the public. We hope that next year will be an even better one and we're looking forward to it with enthusiasm. If we can be of help in regard to National Forest questions, please feel free to stop by or call us. From all of us on the Brasstown Ranger District, Merry Christmas and best wishes for the New Year.

December 20, 1979 –

I've had some people ask about the Christmas tree that is put up every December at our nation's Capitol in Washington, D.C. Where does the tree come from? What kinds of trees are used? When did the program begin? How does the U.S. Forest Service help select the tree?

The Capitol Christmas Tree program began in 1965 with the big push coming from the Speaker of the House at that time, John McCormack. That year, a live Douglas fir tree was selected and actually planted on the Capitol grounds. The thinking was to maintain a living symbol of the Christmas spirit and to re-use the tree in ceremonies each year. Unfortunately, after the 1968 season the tree died.

In 1969 the Forest Service became the agency responsible for the Capitol Christmas Tree program. That year three different trees were pieced together to make the one large tree. The results were not satisfactory. The tree was very difficult to put together and it didn't look that good either.

In 1970 the procedure for selecting the tree was again changed and this procedure has remained in effect since that time. Basically, here's the process:

1) The tree is selected from forests east of the Mississippi River. This involves Regions 8 and 9 of the U.S. Forest Service. The reason for this is that it would be very difficult to transport a large tree from the western United States all the way to the Capitol.

2) Foresters working at the field level are asked to nominate potential trees, based upon size, form, shape, and ease of removing it from the woods.
3) The Architect from the U.S. Capitol, in conjunction with Forest Service officials, makes a final selection and performs an on-the-ground inspection of the tree.
4) The tree is carefully cut, removed from the woods, and transported in one piece to Washington, D.C.

Some local communities have even held going-away ceremonies for "their" tree and the townspeople then accompanied it by caravan to the Capitol.

In 1970 the first tree was selected from the Monongahela National Forest in West Virginia; in 1971 it came from the Cherokee National Forest in Tennessee; and in 1972 it came from the White Mountain National Forest in New Hampshire. I wasn't able to find what species of trees were used during those years.

From 1973 – 1979 the tree species and their sources were:

1973 – White spruce -   Allegheny National Forest (Pennsylvania)

1974 – Fraser fir -   Pisgah National
Forest (North Carolina)
1975 – Balsam fir -   Ottawa National
Forest (Michigan)
1976 – Red spruce -   Monongahela
National Forest (West Virginia)
1977 – White spruce -   Nemadji State
Forest (Minnesota)
1978 – Norway spruce -   Savage River State
Forest (Maryland)
1979 – White spruce -   Nicolet National
Forest (Wisconsin)

    This year's tree was 47 years old and 52 feet tall. The tree was lighted about two weeks before Christmas during a ceremony with several dignitaries attending and the Marine Corps Band playing Christmas music. The tree is usually taken down on January 2.

    The U.S. Forest Service is very proud to help coordinate the Capitol Christmas Tree program. Perhaps someday the Chattahoochee National Forest will furnish our nation's Christmas tree.

December 27, 1979 –

Well, we sure hope everyone had a nice Christmas and that you're looking forward to a happy New Year. It's hard to believe it's almost 1980. Time sure flies.

Here on the Brasstown Ranger District we're looking forward to a very busy year. We have many projects planned, some of which are:

1) Timber Sales – We'll be marking and selling approximately 2.5 million board feet of sawtimber and pulpwood.

2) Firewood – We hope to be able to help meet the ever increasing demand for home fuelwood by having several areas available for gathering firewood. Last year, we issued well over a thousand free firewood permits.

3) Recreation Management – This includes quite a variety of things. We'll be operating two campgrounds – one at Lake Winfield Scott and one at Lake Chatuge. Our recreation program also includes a system of over 40 miles of hiking trails, a small scenic area in Sosebee Cove, patrolling near popular hunting and fishing areas, and maintaining safe access to scenic

waterfalls, such as those at High Shoals and Helton Creek.

4) <u>Visitor Information Services (VIS)</u> – Our most well known VIS effort is operating the Brasstown Bald Visitor Center. This keeps us very busy in the Summer and Fall. Last year, we had over 55,000 visitors from 46 states and 36 foreign countries. The year before that we had about 65,000 visitors, so evidently inflation and the energy crisis convinced some people to stay at home more this past year. Other VIS activities we're involved with are sending out information (maps, brochures, etc.), presenting programs to local schools and organizations, and maintaining a system of informational signs and bulletin boards throughout the District.

5) <u>Wildlife Management</u> – This involves a variety of fish and wildlife habitat improvement work in cooperation with the State Fish and Game Commission.

6) <u>Soil and Water Management</u> – Here we do several acres of soil and/or watershed restoration work. We also have a water quality monitoring program and we're currently conducting soil surveys on

over 40,000 acres of land in Union and surrounding counties.

7) Building Maintenance – One of our continuing jobs is the annual upkeep on all of our buildings (office, work center, recreation areas, visitor center, and residences).

8) Special Use Management – This involves administering over 100 special use permits for such things as road and utility rights-of-way, rock permits, spring boxes, and many other miscellaneous items.

9) Land Lines – We'll be surveying and marking over 10 miles of National Forest boundary lines.

10) Road Maintenance – We annually maintain over 350 miles of roads in Union, Towns, and adjoining counties.

11) Reforestation – We will be planting tree seedlings on over 300 acres of National Forest land.

12) Site Preparation – Many of our employees spend a substantial portion of the year operating chainsaws and other equipment in our old timber sale areas. We prepare the sites for the new, young tree seedlings that need full sunlight in which to grow.

In addition, we have other jobs to do such as prescribed burning, timber stand improvement, campground renovation, and fighting wildfires.

All in all, we have a very busy year ahead of us and we're anxious for it to begin. Once again, we wish everyone a Happy New Year for 1980.

January 3, 1980 –

After the last few days, I'm sure everyone has their cold weather clothing out. I know I sure do. My old coat is my most important piece of Winter clothing. It's a goose down coat that I bought on sale a few years ago when prices weren't so high. It keeps me very warm. My two sons, Jeff and Brent, have vests and coats that they wear which contain the new synthetic fiber-fill material. The boys seem to stay warm, for they never complain about being cold.

This brings up some interesting questions on the relative pros and cons of natural versus the man-made materials.

Natural goose down is probably the most efficient insulating material available for clothing on a pound-for-pound basis. It is very lightweight and easily regains its fluffiness after normal compression. Down also "breathes," and thus body moisture will evaporate quite rapidly, eliminating any dampness problems.

One hint on selecting down clothing is that high quality items are made using prime northern goose down. You can get either duck or goose down, but most experts agree that goose down is the better choice of the two.

On the negative side, down will lose most of its insulating value when it gets wet. It also clumps up and doesn't dry out very fast. The synthetic fiber-fills, however, will still keep much of their insulating value even when wet. They also dry quicker than down items.

For a weight comparison, down sleeping bags might weigh between 2 and 2 ½ pounds, while the synthetic bags might weigh 4 pounds or more. This could be a factor to consider if you plan on taking a long backpacking trip.

As far as cost goes, the synthetic fills are the best buys. For example, a very good goose down coat might cost $70 to $100, while a comparable fiber-fill coat might cost only $45 to $60.

Neither type of insulation can take extremely rough treatment. They both need to be handled carefully – don't wad them up or sit on them; store them by hanging them up; keep them away from moisture; don't store near heat; and make sure you have them cleaned according to instructions on the label.

In summary, if you want more durability and better tolerance to wet weather at a cheaper price, choose the synthetic material. If you want the most warmth and the least weight, choose the goose down. Either way, select your items carefully and enjoy the Winter weather.

January 11, 1980 –

"A country with no regard for its past will have little worth remembering in the future."

These words, spoken by Abraham Lincoln, are very true indeed and a significant portion of man's past in this country is tied strongly to the National Forests.

Like a great history book, your National Forests in the South hold the story of more than 8,000 years of human occupation. Most of us know about the major historical events related to settlement by early French and Spanish colonists, trappers, agriculturists, and loggers. But we seldom realize that over 99 percent of the record of human life in North America was made by countless numbers of people who did not leave a written record – the American Indians.

Without written records we must look for other evidence of the way humans lived in the past, evidence existing on the ground in the form of prehistoric and historic archaeological objects and sites – the physical remains of human behavior. These cultural resources include rock shelters, campsites, petroglyphs, old buildings, pottery, arrow points, stone tools, and historic farmsteads, to name just a few.

Archaeologists can examine these remains and, with many new methods and techniques of recovery and analysis, interpret the past with great accuracy. But once a single object is carelessly removed from a prehistoric or early historic site, the record is damaged and incomplete – much as a book would be incomplete if words were erased or pages torn from it.

The evidence of the past is part of America's cultural heritage, which belongs to all citizens. It is our legacy, left to us by peoples who lived in our land, met the challenge of the environment without modern technology, and left us a cultural heritage which extends back over 10,000 years. This heritage is a precious gift from generations of past Americans.

The Forest Service manages its cultural resources in a manner which recognizes their significance and provides for their protection. The search for information about the history and prehistory of the South is a continuing task. When the Forest Service completes its inventory of cultural resources on National Forest land, it will use the information to clarify the story of human occupation of the South.

In our local area the petroglyphs at Track Rock Gap are a major cultural link with the past. These types of markings are uncommon in the Southeast, and were used by the Cherokees as a landmark in the route from their towns along the Hiwassee River in North Carolina to towns in north Georgia. These carvings are also mentioned by our early settlers and explorers in the accounts of their travels.

Other well known archaeological sites on Georgia's National Forests are Scull Shoals on the Oconee National Forest and an area near Dahlonega of steatite rock outcrops. These rocks were used by Indians around 4,000 years ago to make bowls. The rock is very soft and is fairly easy to carve out. As pottery techniques later developed, the Indians abandoned the steatite rock methods. The Scull Shoals site, on the Oconee River, was a thriving center for manufacturing, trade, and distribution from the late 1700's to the mid 1800's. The town was always dependent on water travel for its commercial growth. As the river silted over and flooding increased, the town declined rapidly and was finally abandoned.

Helping to preserve America's heritage is one of the goals of the Forest Service. You can help preserve America's cultural heritage by leaving archaeological and historical sites undisturbed, encouraging others to do the same, and reporting your discoveries to Forest Service personnel. Collecting artifacts or disturbing sites on National Forest land without written permission is prohibited under the terms of the Federal Antiquities Act of 1906.

As Abraham Lincoln said, preserving our cultural past may well help us to better plan and prepare for the future.

January 16, 1980 –

On January 11th the Brasstown Ranger District held a retirement party at the Union

County Recreation Center in honor of L.A. Rich, who will be taking a well deserved rest after 30 years of government service. Many of his present and past co-workers joined to give L.A. and his wife, Mabel, a big send-off. This included a meal, gifts, many stories, and lots of handshakes and well wishes for a relaxing and enjoyable retirement.

For the past several years L.A. has been our Forestry Technician in charge of Timber Sale Inspections. He also handled various other duties related to the timber program. He's been one of the cornerstones of our District operations for a long time and we'll sure miss him.

Personally, I've learned more about crow hunting from L.A. than I ever thought I'd know. That's one of his passions and, from what everybody tells me, L.A. is one of the best crow hunters around. His future plans include bird hunting, a little farming, making a bunch of sorghum each Fall, and just enjoying life in general.

L.A., we all enjoyed working with you. Good luck in the days ahead. And enjoy that retirement!

On another note: If you watched the Tournament of Roses Parade on TV on New

Year's Day, you probably saw the float with Woodsy Owl and Smokey Bear planting the birthday tree. This was the beginning of the "Plant a Birthday Tree" campaign for 1980 – the 75th birthday of the U.S. Forest Service.

We'll soon be distributing brochures, patches, posters, and other materials advertising the campaign. While the "Plant a Birthday Tree" program will be coordinated on a national level, we'll do some things here, too. If any school group, civic organization, or other group is interested in a tree planting activity, give us a call and we'll set up something.

January 22, 1980 –

An organization like the Forest Service has to have a variety of talented people working for it in order to complete the many jobs that are required. We need skilled and trained workers to do the recreation and timber jobs, the firefighting, the road maintenance, and the building construction and repairs. We need trained people to inventory the natural resources of the forest, prepare work plans, and manage the total District operations. But even with all of the above talented people, we can't run a smooth operation without a capable business management and clerical staff.

Undoubtedly the backbone of our District, the business and clerical staff helps to tie things together so that we can run an efficient overall program. And our people are top notch. Betty Taylor supervises this staff, along with handling most of the financial and personnel matters for our employees (which ranges from 40 in the Winter months to 100 or more in the summertime with our YCC campers.) She also coordinates the requisitions and purchase orders for all of our supplies, materials, and equipment. Betty was featured in an earlier column, so this week I'd like to mention the rest of her staff.

Angie Henson has worked on the Brasstown District for about a year and a half. The first year she was a member of our YACC program, but since then has become Betty's assistant as a regular Forest Service employee. Angie's main duties are timekeeping; making fire reports and keeping fire records; preparing training forms; and keeping leave records for all our employees. Angie has been a tremendous addition to the staff in helping with our heavy workload.

Also, working in our office are Patsy Hughes and Joy Martin. These two young ladies are in our YACC program. Joy started work last March, almost a year ago, and has taken over duties as the main receptionist at our front desk. If you come in the office for a firewood permit, a map, brochures, pamphlets, or just general information, you'll likely be assisted by Joy. She also handles the telephone and radio; answers letters requesting information about the Forest; coordinates our vehicle records and weather data; is responsible for checking in and sending out our daily mail; and she maintains records for our YACC, YCC, and Volunteer programs.

Patsy began work just five months ago and helps out with all of our clerical jobs as part of her training. Her primary duties are general typing and correspondence, filing, routing the mail, record keeping, and also assisting Joy as receptionist.

Along with their specific assigned duties, Angie, Joy, and Patsy handle many other clerical jobs that come up. And they help each other when workloads become heavy.

We all feel we're lucky to have these competent ladies working for us. Along with Betty, they form the backbone of our District – no doubt about it!

January 28, 1980 –

The next couple of weeks I'm busy traveling back and forth to our Supervisor's Office in Gainesville working as a member of the Forest Planning Team. A couple of members of my staff will write this column for me. Today's column is written by Frances Mason, Recreation Forester, who serves as Supervisor of operations at Brasstown Bald Visitor Center.

Have you ever been to Argentina, Czechoslovakia, Japan, or Zambia? Well, people from those countries and others have visited Towns and Union counties during the past year! They were among the 282 people from 36 foreign countries who visited Brasstown Bald Visitor Center last season.

The visitor use figures from 1979 were recently summarized by Mary Young, who serves as our main visitor information specialist at Brasstown Bald in the Summer. She works in our District office during the Winter months. Here are some of the interesting figures she came up with:

1) In 1979 Brasstown Bald VIS Center was visited by 55,590 people. Peak

months were October with 20,959 visitors and August with 9,208.

2) There were 9,525 fewer visitors in 1979 than in 1978. We think this was due to the cold, damp summer and the gas shortage scare.

3) The guest register was signed by 22,254 visitors, which was 40 percent of the total number of visitors.

4) We had visitors from 46 states and the District of Columbia. Hawaii, Idaho, South Dakota, and Wyoming were the missing states. Last year, the only state missing was North Dakota. Would you believe we got North Dakota within the first two weeks this year? There were nine visitors from Alaska and 10 each from Maine and Washington.

5) Of course, the greatest number of visitors came from Georgia – 15,134. Florida came in second with 3,083 and Alabama was third with 683. Rounding out the Top 10 were North Carolina, South Carolina, Tennessee, Ohio, Texas, Mississippi, and Michigan.

6) Four states tied for the fewest number of visitors with two each – Nevada, New Mexico, North Dakota, and Rhode Island.

7) Visitors also came from 36 foreign countries, representing every continent except Antarctica. Here's a surprising fact: the top four countries this year were also the top four last year. Those were England with 76 visitors, Germany – 50, Canada – 25, and Australia – 22. Some of the other top countries represented were: Sweden, Ireland, France, India, Brazil, Turkey, Italy, and Russia.

From these figures you can see that Brasstown Bald draws visitors from all across the United States and from around the world. There probably aren't many other counties the size of Towns and Union that can boast of such a varied guest list.

Brasstown Bald Visitor Center will reopen on March 8 for weekends only until April 26, when it will be open daily. Maybe this will be the year that we get visitors from all 50 states!

February 7, 1980 –

Today's column is written by Debbie Day, who coordinates our youth, senior citizen, and volunteer programs.

With the cold weather we've been having the last couple of weeks, many of you may wonder why this column is about camping. It's true that the majority of people choose to camp and hike in the mountains of the Chattahoochee National Forest during the Spring, Summer, and Fall. But there's also a small group of folks who wait patiently for the forecast of cold temperatures and snow before they pack up and head out on a trail. Why? Most likely for the challenges and solitude that these weather conditions assure them.

One of the first concerns for the Winter camper is keeping warm. Mountain weather is erratic, which requires the mountaineer to be prepared for all possibilities. Temperature changes rapidly with elevation. Temperatures drop about four degrees Fahrenheit for each increase in elevation of 1,000 feet. Thus, going 4,000 feet up a mountain will produce an average drop of 16 degrees.

The two elements common to cold weather with which the camper is most concerned are wind and precipitation. Actually, wind is your enemy and snow is usually your friend. At 30 degrees Fahrenheit a person standing in a calm spot may feel quite warm if wearing sufficient clothing. But turn on a 20 mile an hour wind at the same temperature and you will be quite uncomfortable. The combination of low temperatures and high winds can kill humans and animals alike. If high winds develop, the Winter camper should get out of the wind and sit tight.

On the other hand, snow is like a warm blanket and it can protect the camper from dangerous winds. Piling snow around your tent or digging a snow cave will help insulate humans from Winter storms. However, warm wind or sunshine can turn friendly dry snow into a sloppy mush. A pre-requisite to keeping warm is to stay dry. Wearing proper clothing and packing extra clothes are musts.

The basic thing to keep in mind about clothing is that it acts as thermal insulation; that is, clothes serve to retain body heat. Only the body can actually produce heat through body chemistry involving the release of calories obtained from the food you eat. For Winter camping the daily calorie intake should be about 5,000 calories. A well balanced diet of high energy foods, including fats, is important.

Having the proper clothing, equipment, and food can make the difference between a Winter adventure and Winter disaster. If you are a novice, plan to go with an organized group of experienced Winter campers. There are many skills and tips to be learned that will allow you to enjoy camping in a Winter wonderland.

February 13, 1980 –

The first National Forest established in the eastern United States under the Weeks Law was the Pisgah National Forest in North Carolina, created in 1916. The Weeks Law was passed in 1911 and it provided for the purchase of "forested, cut-over, or divided lands within the watersheds of navigable streams."

Most of the National Forests in the East were purchased from private landowners by the federal government under the Weeks Law. However, most of the National Forests in the West were established from existing government ownership, known as public domain lands. There are a few National Forests in the East that had some public domain lands – the Bankhead in Alabama; the Ocala in

Florida; and the Ozark and the Ouachita in Arkansas.

After the Pisgah in 1916, the next eastern National Forests were established in 1918 - the George Washington in Virginia; the Jefferson in Virginia; and the White Mountain in New Hampshire.

Beginning in 1920 there was a major effort to establish National Forest lands throughout the Appalachian Mountains. Lands were purchased in North Carolina, South Carolina, Georgia, Tennessee, Virginia, West Virginia, and Pennsylvania.

From these modest beginnings arose the eastern National Forests, which have become so important to all of us. Generally speaking, in the western United States there are fewer high population centers than in the East. And there is a lot of public land in the West, plenty of land for westerners for camping, hiking, fishing, and outdoor recreation pursuits.

But in the East, with more population and less public land, these areas become extremely valuable and important. Because of this many people consider the eastern National Forests to be more "valuable" than the western National Forests.

Whether you agree with that or not, our eastern forests continue to be in demand for more types of uses and greater activity than at any time in the past. Because of this the Forest Service undertakes orderly and organized long-range planning on these forests.

Be sure to let your voice be heard in telling us how you think your .... Chattahoochee National Forest should be managed.

February 23, 1980 –

Most people are aware of the major jobs the Forest Service performs – fire fighting, timber management, operating campgrounds, and so forth. But we're also involved in many other activities from coast to coast which vary a little bit from our standard duties.

An example of this occurred recently in California. The Forest Service joined with several other agencies – the U.S. Fish and Wildlife Service, the Bureau of Land Management, and the California Department of Fish and Game – along with the National Audubon Society, in signing an agreement to protect the California condor.

This agreement initiated a more extensive program to protect the endangered bird than has ever been undertaken before. At present, there are only about 25 to 30 California condors left in the wild and most of those make their homes in the Los Padres National Forest. Hopefully, an all out effort by these agencies and groups can save this large bird from extinction.

All across the country the Forest Service gets involved in a variety of projects to help protect our environment and to improve our resource management capability.

Here are a couple of interesting notes I came across last week:

1) Worldwide there are 333,000 new births per day and 124,000 deaths per day. This equals 209,000 additions per day or about 76,285,000 additions per year.

2) By about 1830 there were approximately one billion people in the world; by 1930 there were an estimated two billion. By 1960, just 30 years later, the number was three billion; and it took just 15 more years, until 1975, to reach four billion.

Numbers like these make you sit back and think about the great demands that are being placed upon all of our natural resources – water, air, agriculture, forests, wildlife and others. Wise use of our resources and thoughtful long-range planning are musts for the future.

Employee Spotlight – Mary Young has worked for the U.S. Forest Service since January 1971. Mary grew up in Towns County and graduated from Towns County High School. Her first job at the Chattahoochee National Forest was as a clerk-typist. She also handled some purchasing, maintained timber sale records, and filled in at Brasstown Bald Visitor Center when needed. In the Summer of 1974 she began working at Brasstown Bald full time. She now works on the mountain from the time we open in March until the time we close, usually around December 1st. Her Winter months are spent in the office assisting with a variety of jobs and compiling and keeping records from the previous season at Brasstown Bald.

Mary is a tremendous asset to our District organization. She particularly enjoys meeting and talking with people from all over the country and world who come to visit Brasstown Bald. Mary and her family live on West Union near Young Harris.

February 28, 1980 –

<u>Notes From Here and There</u>

- Our Brasstown Bald Visitor Center will be opening up on March 8 and March 9. It will just be open on weekends until April 28, at which time we begin daily operations. While we're on the weekend schedule, the hours of operation will be from 10:00 a.m. – 5:30 p.m. We hope you all get a chance to visit Brasstown Bald this Spring or Summer.
- The Appalachian Trail in Georgia was originally scouted and blazed in 1929 by Roy Ozmer. In the late Winter of 1936 there was a work project on the entire length of the Georgia section. The Forest Service was involved quite often in the trail work. During the war the trail was used very little and it became overgrown. Then, in 1946 the Forest Service marked and cleared the entire length of the trail in the Chattahoochee National Forest. Since that time there has been great cooperation between the Georgia

Appalachian Trail Club and the Forest Service in maintaining the trail.

- There are plans in the works for a new hiking trail which will run from Springer Mountain, Georgia to Davenport Gap in the Great Smokey Mountain National Park. The trail will go through Georgia, Tennessee, and North Carolina and will be about 238 miles in length. The trail will be called the Benton MacKaye National Recreation Trail, in honor of the "father" of the Appalachian Trail. The new trail will tie in to the Appalachian Trail in North Carolina and the Perimeter Trail in the Great Smokies, thus allowing hikers to make a loop back to Springer Mountain without having to retrace any of their steps. It will be the longest loop trail in the Southeast. The proposed route is 95 percent on public land. When finished, the trail will be managed jointly by the Forest Service and the Park Service.
- Water shortages are being predicted by the 1990's, especially in the West and Midwest. This is about half the

total area of the lower 48 states. There are many implications in this prediction that could affect our lifestyles and living conditions. Our nation's forests will become increasingly important as the headwaters for most streams. Pure, clean water is one of the most important products of a well managed forest. The Forest Service is actively involved in research that will help improve the quality and quantity of water that comes from National Forest land.

March 7, 1980 –

Today's column is written by Debbie Day, who coordinates our Senior Citizen Program on the Brasstown Ranger District, Chattahoochee National Forest.

Forest Service Honors Older Workers

March 9 – 15 is <u>National Employ the Older Worker Week.</u> This is an annual event sponsored by the American Legion to promote employment of older workers. Besides reminding employers of work-related skills and maturity to be found among unemployed and under-employed older workers, this campaign informs middle-aged and older job seekers of available year-round assistance through the public employment service.

As our society has changed, it has become increasingly difficult for older people to find productive and challenging jobs. To help, Congress passed the Older American Act in 1971, which established the Senior Community Service Employment Program (SCSEP). Locally, the Forest Service became a sponsor in 1972.

Our SCSEP program seeks to provide a supplemental income for senior citizens; allow older folks to utilize their skills, experience, and wisdom; and provide work experience and training that will encourage employers to hire more senior workers.

The Brasstown Ranger District presently employs seven Older American workers. Their ages range from 63 to 77 years old. Our workers include: Harley Anderson with eight years of service; Marshall Dellinger with six years of service; Marlor Garrett with eight years of service; Floyd Ledford with four years of service; Frank Thompson with eight years of service; Talmadge Rogers with eight years of service; and Georgia Sullivan with six years of service.

Dellinger, Anderson, and Garrett are assigned to our road crew, which maintains 290 miles of road each year. Rogers, Thompson, and Ledford are assigned to our recreation and building maintenance crew, which is responsible for the ship-shape appearance of our recreation facilities. Sullivan works in our District office doing cleaning and clerical work.

On March 7 each Older American was recognized at our monthly safety meeting. Each person was presented a Certificate of Appreciation for their dedicated service in helping the Forest Service maintain our nation's natural resources.

March 12, 1980 –

Today's column is written by Al Vanderpoel, a friend of mine who is a Civil Engineer with the U.S. Forest Service. Al and I worked together on the Wayne National Forest in Ohio during the years 1975-1977. He has worked at three or four national forests and is currently assigned to the Nicolet National Forest in Wisconsin. This column explains some of the contrasts

*between the Nicolet and Chattahoochee
National Forests and points out some of the
attractions in the North Country. I hope you
enjoy reading it.*

It was 26 degrees below zero last night –
our coldest day of the Winter thus far. Nothing
moves outside unless it absolutely has to at that
temperature. Up to two feet of snow is on the
ground, but last night it was too cold for it to
snow any more. This morning the ice on my
path to work literally groaned as I walked over
it.

I'll bet you are asking why anyone would
want to live in a place like this. Well, I'm
writing from the Nicolet National Forest and,
believe it or not, there are people here who
would have nothing else. The Nicolet is in
northern Wisconsin and predictably, because
of the harsh climate, it is still sparsely
populated. There are a lot of remote areas here
with only trees and lakes. It's not true
wilderness like you might find in northern
Minnesota or Canada, but we have one area
where you can drive for 23 miles without
seeing a house.

That's the one major reason why a lot of
the local people live here; they like a place that
is not too crowded. But there are other reasons

as well. This is a sportsman's paradise, with deer and other game plentiful; the fishing is great; and there are miles and miles of snowmobile and hiking trails. The area is known for its many lakes – in fact, there are 1168 lakes within the boundaries of the Nicolet. And while there are no mountains here, or even any good sized hills, the countryside is rolling. By walking only a few miles, you can cross several smaller hills and see many new views. Around every corner there is a stream or lake or swamp or a new stand of timber.

The timber is exceptionally good; it grows fast; and the lumber industry is strong here. Before the area was settled, the forests consisted primarily of huge white pine trees; some of these stands still remain as a reminder of those days. In fact, the largest eastern white pine in the United States is here – 148 feet tall and 67 inches in diameter. Today, a diversity of northern tree species covers the land.

Getting back to the weather, 26 below zero may make you shiver just reading about it, but I would bet that zero degrees in Georgia feels colder. The cold here in Wisconsin is very dry with little wind; and by dressing warmly the cold will hardly bother you. Winter sports are well promoted here, including a snowshoe baseball league! We had a short thaw recently, which is very unusual, and while folks sometimes complain about the cold, the loudest complaints came from people who couldn't cross country ski or ice skate for a week.

Yes, the temperatures here are cold, and the Winters are long, but the local people love it. My wife and I have adjusted, too. So long from Wisconsin. We hope to visit your beautiful north Georgia mountains, which Dan and Vicki have told us so much about, either this summer or next.

March 20, 1980 –

Last Fall, the local newspaper was unable to run one of my historical columns about the early days of forestry in this country. Today and next week, I will re-do some of that "missing" column and add a few years, providing highlights in the history of forestry from 1890 to 1897. These years saw activities increase which helped to conserve and protect our country's forest resources.

1890 – The cutting of 20 million board feet of green timber annually on the Menominee Indian Reservation in Wisconsin was authorized by an Act of Congress. This was the first federal law regulating cutting of live timber on government-managed lands.

Sequoia, Yosemite, and General Grant National Parks were created, all in the Sierra Mountains of California. Total area at first was 838,770 acres; eventually this was nearly doubled by the addition of lands from adjacent forest reserves and national forests. The name of the General Grant park was later changed to Kings Canyon National Park, which was eventually combined with the Sequoia National Park.

1891 – By an Act of Congress, approved March 3, 1891, the President was given power to establish forest reserves from public domain land (26 Stat. 1103). The provision was attached as a rider to a bill revising the public land laws. This was the beginning of the National Forest System. The first lands reserved are now in the Shoshone and Teton National Forests. On October 16, President Harrison signed a proclamation withdrawing 1,198,080 acres in Colorado, known as the White River Plateau Timberland Reserve, now in the White River National Forest. Before his term expired, President Harrison set aside forest reservations totaling 13 million acres. No plan of operation was passed by Congress, so the reserves were simply "closed" areas.

North Carolina set up a Forest Inquiry Commission.

Maine authorized its State Land Agent to serve also as State Forest Commissioner with the duty to collect data on forest fire losses, forest waste, and on the reduction of forest area as to its effect on watersheds.

March 25, 1980 –

Continuing from last week –
1892 – President Harrison proclaimed eight more Timberland Reserves: Pike's Peak, Plum Creek, South Platte, and Battlement Mesa, all in Colorado; Pecos River in New Mexico; Bull Run in Oregon; San Gabriel in California; and Afognak in Alaska.

Gifford Pinchot was employed as the first professional American Forester, on the Biltmore Estate of George W. Vanderbilt in the mountains of western North Carolina.

1893 – New Hampshire set up a State Forestry Commission with responsibility for forestry education as well as authority to purchase land for public purposes.

Five more timberland reserves were set aside by President Harrison: Sierra, San Bernardino, and Trabuco Canyon in California; Pacific in Washington; and Grand Canyon in Arizona for a total of 13.5 million acres during his administration. President Grover Cleveland created the Cascade Range and Ashland Timberland Reserves in Oregon, aggregating over 4.5 million acres.

1895 – Pennsylvania created the office of State Commissioner of Forestry.

Dr. Carl A. Schenck succeeded Pinchot as Forester on the Biltmore Estate.

1897 – President Cleveland, just before the close of his term, proclaimed more than 20 million acres of new reserves. Soon after, Congress passed an act of organization and management for those public forests. It authorized the hiring of employees to administer the forests and made possible the opening of the reserves for use. This Act of June 4, with later amendments, is the one under which the National Forests are now being administered. (Until 1905, the General Land Office in the Department of Interior was in charge. The Division of Forestry gave only technical advice. The Geologic Survey was assigned the duty for surveying and mapping of the forests.)

Pennsylvania law provided for the state acquisition of tax delinquent lands to become State Forest Reserves.

April 3, 1980 –

Frances Mason wrote today's column. She serves as Recreation Forester on the Brasstown Ranger District.

The people who will be working at Brasstown Bald Visitor Center this Summer recently visited the Cradle of Forestry in America, a visitor center and recreation facility in North Carolina. We were all impressed and highly recommend a trip there to anyone. Let me tell you about our visit, which also served as a training session for us. Many of the ideas we got from our trip will be put to use at Brasstown Bald in the future.

The facility was built by and is operated by the U.S. Forest Service, Pisgah National Forest. It re-creates the first forestry school in America and is located about 14 miles outside of Brevard, North Carolina about 30 miles from Asheville.

Our visit to the Cradle began at the Visitor Center, where a 20-minute film explained the history of the forestry school, which began in 1898. At that time the land belonged to George Vanderbilt, builder and owner of the famous Biltmore House near Asheville. Vanderbilt imported Dr. Carl Schenck, a college trained Forester from Germany, to manage his Pisgah Forest. Schenck acquired a following of young men interested in forestry and soon found himself teaching forestry, as well as managing the land. The film shows what it was like to study and work with Dr. Schenck as well as to live in the mountains at the turn of the century.

The Visitor Center also contains forestry-oriented exhibits and artifacts from the early 1900's.

From the Visitor Center we took a mile-long hike along a paved pathway leading through a rhododendron filled forest to eight buildings. Some of these are the actual buildings used by Dr. Schenck and his students and some are reproductions of the original buildings. The movie we saw was filmed in and around these buildings.

The first stop on the trail was the combination church and school house where the forestry students got their "book learnin'." The building was reconstructed in 1966 with funds donated by the alumni of the Biltmore Forest School.

Other stops along the way included the commissary – a store and meeting place for students and local mountaineers; the Ranger's dwelling, where some of the students were boarders; Schenck's office, which he made from half of an abandoned barn; a Black Forest Lodge; the blacksmith's shop; the student quarters; and another Black Forest Lodge.

The Black Forest Lodges are the original buildings which Schenck had local people build for his Rangers to live in. They were named after the Black Forest of Germany because Schenck had them built in the style of architecture he remembered from back home. The picturesque lodges look like something out of a story book. The second lodge houses a small store which sells postcards and a variety of books on forestry-related topics.

Many of the buildings have push button recordings that explain the structure and what it was used for. All of the buildings are furnished as authentically as possible.

We also got a sneak preview of a new trail that will be opening around the first of June. The Forest Festival Trail will be about one mile long and will have 15 stops, including a sawmill, an old logging train, and various research plots. These plots are small scale reproductions of the research plots that Schenck located throughout the Pisgah Forest.

The Cradle of Forestry is located in a valley called the Pink Beds because of the abundance of rhododendron. Try to plan your visit to the Cradle during the early part of June when the rhododendron will be in full bloom. If you like the natural beauty of the forest and historical places, you can't help but enjoy a trip to the Cradle of Forestry in America.

April 17, 1980 –

With the arrival of Spring, we know that our heavy-use recreation season is just around the corner. Even with the uncertainty created by the energy shortage, we're expecting a very busy summer. We're geared up and ready to go at Brasstown Bald Visitor Center and Lake Chatuge Campground. However, Lake Winfield Scott Campground will not be open to campers this Summer, due to a major reconstruction project. People may still fish, swim, and picnic (only in the beach area.)

The campground at Lake Winfield Scott will be getting a new look over the next year. The layout of the campground itself will be revised to improve its appearance and to better distribute the users. A few projects have already been completed and many more are scheduled. Here are the highlights of our reconstruction and rehabilitation plan for Lake Winfield Scott:

1) The entire road system will be re-done. This will include new paving and relocation of some sections. This project is now in progress. The safety hazard created by the use of heavy machinery is the primary reason for closing the area to camping until the project is completed.

2) The entrance to the campground itself will be moved from its present location to a point approximately ¼ mile south on Highway 180. The present entrance is near a sharp curve and at the end of a bridge. This safety problem will be corrected by the new location.

3) New signs will be placed at the entrance and throughout the campground.

4) Just inside the entrance, future plans call for a new entry station; a little further in, there will be a dump station for sanitary disposal of wastes.

5) The present entrance will be blocked off about 200 feet in, and this section will

be used as a parking area for fishermen. We'll build a dock just below the present entry building where these fishermen can launch canoes and small boats.

6) There will be approximately 41 campsites in the campground after the reconstruction, complete with new spurs, tent pads, firegrates, etc.

7) The old bath house at the swimming beach was remodeled last summer.

8) All roads and campsites will be revegetated and reseeded.

9) Future plans also call for an amphitheatre, which will feature a view out over the lake.

We're sorry for any inconveniences that may arise because of the construction project, but please try to bear with us. The above items will improve the appearance of the campground and help us provide the Forest visitor with a more enjoyable visit.

If you should have any questions, please call us at the District Office in Blairsville at 745-6928.

April 25, 1980 –

The first part of this column ran about a year ago. I have added more information about our current effort to prepare a Forest Plan for the Chattahoochee and Oconee National Forests. I am a member of the Planning Team working on this project and we sincerely want your input and ideas for the future management of your...... national forest.

There are 187 million acres of National Forest land in the United States, including Puerto Rico. This includes land in every state except Iowa, Maryland, Delaware, New Jersey, Connecticut, Rhode Island, and Massachusetts. Ownership of these lands is vested with the approximately 219 million citizens of this country. That figures out to be just over 4/5 of an acre per person.

If you had your say, how would you want the Forest Service to manage your 4/5 of an acre?

Or, how would you want all of the 187 million acres of National Forests managed?

More realistically, how would you like to see your favorite National Forest or Forests managed? This could be the Chattahoochee-Oconee in Georgia, the Nantahala in North

Carolina, the Sumter in South Carolina, or the Cherokee in Tennessee. Or you might have some particular interest in the Ocala in Florida, the Bitterroot in Montana, or the Allegheny in Pennsylvania.

The 187 million acres of National Forests represent a treasury of many things. The American people use these Forests for camping, hiking, fishing, hunting, watersheds, grazing, timber, wilderness, wildlife, and many other important things.

Which, and how much, of the desired products and uses these lands will supply must be determined well ahead of time. Forests cannot be hurried. Thus, each National Forest will be preparing a Land Management Plan which will outline how the Forest will be managed over a 10-year period. These plans will be completed no later than 1985.

The Chattahoochee-Oconee Plan is scheduled for completion by mid-1982, so we're already heavily involved in gathering data and public input. We're trying to get as much public input as possible by the first of May (no later than the end of June), so that we can begin working on possible solutions to your issues and concerns. However, any time that you have comments in the next two years, please feel free to present them to the Forest Service.

With the public's help we can prepare a Land Management Plan that will be acceptable to everyone concerned. You can provide your comments and input at any District Office or the Supervisor's Office in Gainesville. District Office locations are: Blairsville, LaFayette, Clarkesville, Dahlonega, Chatsworth, Clayton, Blue Ridge, and Monticello.

As I have previously mentioned, I am a member of the Forest Planning Team and have been traveling back and forth frequently between Blairsville and Gainesville. Adding this responsibility to my already heavy workload has made it difficult to always write this weekly column. Thank goodness other employees, most notably Frances Mason, Debbie Day and Martin Kindred, have stepped forward to help me with that task. We want to keep this column going because it is such a good way to communicate with the local citizens who live near the National Forest. And there has been much positive feedback from readers, too. Thanks goes out to all of you for your continued interest in the Chattahoochee National Forest.

In the years leading up to 1900 the forest conservation movement began to expand greatly under the dynamic leadership of Gifford Pinchot. Pinchot brought the word "conservation" into popular usage, as "the wise use of natural resources." The next two decades saw the establishment of a forestry profession. The Forest Service came into being. The National Forest System, that is, the idea of "National Forests," was developed and expanded. All of these things were directly a result of Pinchot's leadership and foresight.

1898 – Gifford Pinchot was named head of the Forestry Division in the U.S. Department of Agriculture with a staff of 12 people – six for clerical/record keeping and six for scientific work. Within seven years the number of employees had increased to more than 700, many of them graduates of the newly established forestry schools. It was in 1898 that the first field work was done by U.S. Forestry employees. The field work consisted of special investigations in connection with illegal lumbering. Pinchot, with great energy and leadership, enlarged and extended the scope of the Division of Forestry beyond the confines of the office to make it a vital and useful service.

The first 4-year professional curriculum in Forestry was started at Cornell University in New York. In the same year the Biltmore Forestry School, a private school, was started in North Carolina. The Yale Forest School was established in 1900, offering a graduate curriculum in Forestry leading to a Masters Degree. During the next five years, regular Forestry curricula were started at the Universities of Michigan, Maine, Nebraska, and Minnesota; the State Forest Academy at Mont Alto, PA; and Colorado College. Harvard University set up an undergraduate curriculum in 1903, but later moved its forest work to the graduate school. Before 1905, Michigan State and Iowa State colleges also were also offering non-professional courses that later were expanded into full professional curricula.

The first Farmer's Bulletin on Forestry was issued, entitled "Forestry for the Farmers."

The General Land Office grouped the Forest Reserves into 11 Districts, each headed by a Superintendent. Each Reserve was under the direction of a Supervisor, who was assisted by Rangers who conducted forest patrols, forest protection, and other work as needed.

1899 – The Act of February 28, 1899 provided for recreational use of the Forest Reserves. This was the first of such laws to recognize the value of the forests for recreation. Later laws extended the uses permitted and provided for regulations to keep the facilities always available to the people.

Minnesota set up a State Forestry Board and designated as Forest Reserves all tracts set aside or acquired by the state or donated to the state for forestry purposes.

Michigan set up a State Forestry Commission.

Mt. Ranier National Park was established in Washington State on 239,892 acres taken from the Pacific Forest Reserve.

1900 – The Society of American Foresters, a professional organization of technically trained Foresters, was founded.

May 7, 1980 –

Today's column is written by Martin Kindred, Forester on the Brasstown Ranger District.

Spring has sprung, the days are getting longer, Memorial Day weekend is just around the corner.....the Summer vacation season is almost here.

For their vacations many people like to visit the parks and recreation areas managed by the federal government. Some of these areas charge fees for entrance, use, and special recreation permits as authorized by the Federal Recreation Fee Program under the Land and Water Conservation Fund Act of 1965.

Also, as part of the Federal Recreation Fee Program, the Golden Eagle Passport and the Golden Age Passport were established. Both of these can reduce the expense of visiting the parks and recreation areas, especially for senior citizens; if several visits are planned; or if a large family is involved.

The Golden Eagle Passport is for persons under 62 years of age. It is an annual entrance permit to parks, national monuments, and recreation areas administered by the federal government. It admits the permit holder and a carload of accompanying people. Where entry is not by private car, the Golden Eagle Passport admits the permit holder and family group – parents, children, spouse, etc. The Golden Eagle Passport does not cover use fees, such as fees for camping and other special use charges; it is valid for entrance fees only.

The Golden Eagle Passport costs $10 and is not refundable or transferable. It is good for one calendar year.

The Golden Age Passport is for persons 62 years of age and older. It is a free lifetime entrance permit to those parks, monuments, and recreation areas administered by the federal government which charge entrance fees. It also provides for a 50 percent discount on federal use fees charged for facility rentals (like picnic shelters), camping, boat launching, parking, etc. The Golden Age Passport does not cover fees charged by private concessionaires working under contract to the government.

The Golden Age Passport admits the permit holder and a carload of accompanying people. Where entry is not by private car, the Golden Age Passport admits the permit holder and his or her spouse and children.

You may only obtain a Golden Age Passport in person, not by mail. You must show proof of age, such as with a state driver's license showing your birth date or a birth certificate. Medicare cards are not acceptable. If you have no proof of age, you must sign an affidavit attesting to your age.

The Golden Age Passport is available at most federally operated recreation areas where it may be used. Thus, it may not be necessary to obtain the Passport before beginning a vacation trip.

The Golden Eagle Passport is available at our Blairsville Office and must be obtained in person. If you want information on other offices where this may be purchased, we have that. Call us at 404-745-6928 or 6929.

May you all have a wonderful Summer and safe, enjoyable vacations.

May 14, 1980 –

Spring is a wonderful time in the Appalachian Mountains. The hills and valleys seem to come alive after their long Winter's rest. Though Fall has always been my favorite season of the year, there is something special about Spring that seems to refresh everyone.

In the mountains we have a variety of native trees that burst into early color, often even before Winter is even quite over. These colorful eye-pleasers include redbud, dogwood, silverbell, pin cherry, red maple, and serviceberry.

The serviceberry, or "sarvus" tree, is one of the most beautiful of our native trees. It is among the earliest of our Spring blooming woody plants, with its pretty white flowers blooming soon after the first warm weather. The white blossoms dot the landscape in late

March or early April and often last for over a month. By summertime the "sarvus" produces a fruit, which is edible and is eaten by birds, wild animals, and people. The fruit, which resembles little apples, makes excellent jelly. Most all of my kinfolk back in the mountains of West Virginia have made sarvus jelly.

There is an old mountain tale which explains how the serviceberry got its name. Back in the early days of settling the Appalachian Mountains, families would settle in certain hollows and pretty much live and die there. Most major hollows had their own church, school house, and maybe a small general store. Many mountain people only went into the larger towns a couple of times a year.

Circuit preachers generally made the "rounds" giving church services over a wide area. Mostly these services were given in the Spring, Summer, and early Fall because in the old days Winter travel was either difficult or impossible in most mountain locations.

So, if there were any deaths during the Winter months, there was no preacher available to perform the funeral. Since the Appalachians stay fairly cold all Winter long, there was no problem storing the bodies in a cold place until the Spring thaw. By then, the circuit preacher was able to start back on his rounds, giving several burial services. The ground was thawed enough, too, so that digging a grave was no problem.

Well, normally by the time the preacher gave his first burial "sarvus" each Spring, the pretty, white-flowered tree was beginning to bloom, hence the name serviceberry or sarvus.

I first heard this story in my native West Virginia mountains and I'm fairly certain there's some truth to it for all of the Appalachian Mountain areas. There are many, many common names throughout our mountains which originated like the serviceberry – by association with some common happening or event.

May 20, 1980 –

Ramps – one of nature's true pleasures. I promised not to write about these tasty little morsels this Spring, but I just can't help it. Ramps are perhaps the best food found in the woods. I will concede to you bird hunters that ramps may rank number two behind grouse, but I rate ramps ahead of fish, deer meat, blackberries, mushrooms (even morels), and any other wild food that I can think of.

You need to eat ramps and judge them according to their taste, not according to the stories you've heard about them, and not according to how they smell on your breath. Just roll the little devils around on your tongue about twice. Then chomp down into sheer eating ecstasy. Um-Umm! It makes my mouth water.

We ate ramps growing up in West Virginia. Dad loved them. I ate them when I worked on the Wayne National Forest in southern Ohio. I did miss them for the two years we lived in Minnesota. I wasn't sure what to expect when I moved to Georgia, but Odell Ballew came to the rescue. He took me to one of his favorite ramp patches and I was back in business. Thank you Odell!

Again this year, I'll describe my two favorite ways to eat ramps. The first way is to cut the leaves off, dip the bulbs into batter, and deep fry them. Put a little ketchup on them and you'll have a treat better than any French fried onion ring you've ever eaten. And for those of you who are breath conscious, deep frying ramps takes some of the "nip" out of them.

My second favorite way is to eat the ramps raw, along with a plate of cornbread and beans. Now I mean to tell you, if you can find something better to eat than a meal of cornbread, beans, and ramps, I'd sure like to know what it is! The only rule is to never take more than two bites of beans or cornbread without eating at least one ramp.

You'll have to excuse how excited I get when I talk about ramps, but I can't help it. I first ate ramps at an early age back home in West Virginia. Dad and I dug 'em, Mom prepared 'em, and we all ate 'em. Thanks, Mom and Dad, for getting me off to a good start!

Well, if you'll excuse me, it's lunch time. I think I'll go home to eat. And have some.....you know what.

May 27, 1980 –

We were talking about Spring the other day and about how glad we were that Winter was now well behind us. It brought to mind an old story I'd heard while I was a kid. I think you'll enjoy it.

As you all know, the Appalachian Mountains from north Georgia to my native West Virginia and beyond can receive lots of snowfall and harsh weather conditions. In fact it gets downright wicked at times. (Our New England and other northern neighbors may not realize that, but it's true nevertheless.) Well, anyway, back to the story.

In pre-Civil War days, roads thru the mountains were few and far between. And what roads there were had to pass thru high mountain gaps and passes on the way to the low country. But there was mail service in those days, too. The mailmen traveled the old trails, wagon roads, and dirt turnpikes. Along these roads there were scattered inns, taverns, and coach houses.

Late one Fall a new mail carrier took over a mountain route. While staying at an Inn one night, a storm came up and he became snowbound. Well, the story goes that after one or two failed attempts to cross the mountain, he came to enjoy the hospitality at the Inn so well that he decided to stay for the Winter. And it just kept snowing.

After a time, the people on the other end of the mail route started to get impatient. Finally, they were able to get word out, along the coast, and on to Washington, D.C. Soon a tracer was sent out to locate the missing carrier, and more importantly, his mail. Thereupon, he wrote a famous letter (which hangs framed in Washington, D.C.), addressed to the Postmaster General of the United States.

The letter explained what had happened and it ended by saying, "If the floodgates of hell were to open, and it were to rain fire and brimstone for six straight weeks, it wouldn't melt all the snow on this mountain. So, if the flatlanders want their blamed old mail, let them come and get it!"

This is a true story and I can believe every word of it. These Appalachian Mountains have spawned a lot of tales and folklore, many of which are among the most colorful in this country. It's a great heritage and I'm very proud of my "mountain roots."

June 4, 1980 –

When people talk about colorful Spring trees and beautiful ornamental trees, they generally speak of dogwood, redbud, serviceberry, or other such common beauties. However, when you come to think about it, there's one tree that offers as much year-round color to the forest as any other species. It's the often overlooked red maple.

As Spring comes forth in the mountains, part of the early color is brought on by the red maple, as the reddish flowers emerge onto the bare limbs. Where there are several red maples growing close together, the Spring color is as beautiful as the serviceberry.

In the Fall the leaves of the red maple turn a brilliant scarlet and are among the prettiest in the woods. The bark of the red maple is a smooth gray color on the younger trees. When growing in clumps, these trees are very pretty, offering a pleasing contrast to the rough bark of the oaks and pines.

The red maple grows throughout eastern North America and is perhaps our most widely spread tree. They are found in Canada, as well as southern Florida, which indicates the tree adapts well to various growing conditions.

The wing-like seeds of the red maple are blown for quite long distances, which enables the species to seed-in over quite an area. Also, when the larger trees are cut, the stumps produce clusters of fast-growing sprouts that can almost dominate certain sites.

Red maple is one of those trees that isn't particularly loved by anyone, but in truth is one of our most abundant and important species. It grows fast and vigorously, but isn't especially valuable as a timber tree. Its wood is somewhat soft and weak, and is sold as "soft maple." (The sugar maple is a more valuable timber tree and is sold as "hard maple." It is not common this far south, however).

Red maple timber commonly goes into cheaper furniture, crates, pallets, pulpwood, etc. The wood is often defective, and many of the trees over 20 inches in diameter are culls. Red maple is very susceptible to wounds and rot. Because of its thin bark, it can be killed by ground fires.

Red maple has been planted in several towns and cities as an ornamental and shade tree. It doesn't grow extremely large and has an attractive, tight crown.

As a food for wildlife, the red maple is excellent. Browsing animals, such as deer, love to eat the tender sprouts (which are also red in color); squirrels and chipmunks feed on the seeds; and several birds, including grouse, find the buds to be a tasty treat.

The red maple may not be our most important timber tree; it may not be the preferred food for all wildlife species; and you may have a tree you think is more colorful. But considering its many qualities and its wide range, the red maple is definitely one of our most valuable all-around tree species.

June 11, 1980 –

We've had quite a few people come in to the office lately and ask about camping in National Forest areas that are not developed campgrounds. Basically, camping is allowed on almost all sections of the Chattahoochee National Forest. There are a few rules and guidelines that need to be followed however:

1) Camping is allowed (without a fee) on all areas, unless otherwise posted. Exceptions would be developed campgrounds (a fee is required at those), boat launching areas, archaeological sites, picnic areas, or any other "special" areas.

2) Any garbage, cans, bottles, or other litter must be taken out when you leave.

3) If camping in a designated Wilderness Area, there may be special requirements such as getting a permit at the local Ranger Station. If you're planning on camping in a Wilderness Area, check at the office for details.

4) Dispose of human waste at least 100 feet from any water. Dig a small hole 6 to 8 inches deep and then cover it up. Natural bacterial decomposition will take place.

5) Dispose of all waste water and wash water away from lakes, streams, and springs. Boil or treat all water before drinking it.

6) Bring your own tent poles and stakes. Don't cut live tree limbs and boughs to sleep on. It is illegal to cut or dig any live vegetation. This includes small brush and shrubs, as well as trees.

7) Firewood cannot be cut down. You can only use dead and down wood that you find laying on the ground. Firewood is scarce in many areas. Therefore, for cooking we recommend taking a small, portable stove with you.

8) If you must have a campfire, keep it safe and small. Shelter it from wind and keep it away from nearby logs, brush, and trees. Clear out a small circle to mineral soil in which to build your fire. If available, put a ring of rocks around it. When you're done, make sure the fire is dead out. Scatter the rocks and cover the black, burned circle with leaves and twigs. Several of these black circles in a small area can be very unsightly.

9) Plan your trip. Know the area and the predicted weather. Carry extra clothes, a map, a first aid kit, and a compass. Be

sure that a friend or relative knows where you'll be, in case of emergencies.

Follow these few simple rules and you can enjoy a camping trip on almost any area of the Chattahoochee National Forest.

June 20, 1980 –

My friend Ray Schoener is the Timber Management Assistant Ranger on the Ironton Ranger District, Wayne National Forest in Ohio. Other people here at our office in Blairsville were either gone this week or tied up with work projects, so I asked Ray if he would write this week's column for me. I hope you enjoy what he has to say about rain and water.

How many times have you looked outside from the comfort of your living room and noticed that the sky had suddenly clouded up and a soft rain or drizzle had started to fall? You probably grumbled to yourself and to anyone within sight that there was another day shot; that your plans for a picnic, or drive, or shopping would have to be postponed until later.

That's happened to all of us, I'm sure. But we somehow survived the wiles of nature and put it out of our minds until the next time it happened.

A perpetual outdoors, consisting of nothing but sun and warm weather, and certainly no rain, snow, or sleet, would be the answer to many people's prayers. But most people know that is not realistic and just put up with the inconvenience of precipitation. It's a bother to them, but they figure it's just part of life.

And how right they are! For without water there would be no life of any kind. Animals and humans need water. And certainly plants do, too. The leaves of trees, grasses, and shrubs need water for photosynthesis. That is the process in which leaves trap radiant energy from the sun and use it for power to make carbohydrates from water and carbon dioxide. And without the carbohydrates there would be no food for man or animals; no wood for shelter; no humus for the soil; and no deposits of coal or oil would have ever developed.

Man and animals need water for other basic needs. Animals need it for drinking; some need it for their homes; some for protection; and some for rearing their young. Man needs it for drinking and bathing, and also for crops, for industries, transportation, medicine, household needs, public sanitation, and recreation.

While it's true that sometimes nature pours more precipitation on us than we need, and the timing may interfere with personal plans, we can take some consolation out of knowing that the rain is doing some good somewhere. It may be for the farmer and his crops or for his pond, which is beneficial for both his stock and for wild animals and aquatic creatures. And the rain is certainly good for natural vegetation.

The song "Raindrops Keep Falling on My Head" implies that when it rains, nothing is right. But with apologies to that songwriter, it's just not so.

June 25, 1980 –

Goodbyes are kind of hard for me, so I usually make them short and sweet. This week's column, my last, will be no exception.

You see, I'll shortly be transferring to the Wayne National Forest in southeastern Ohio, near the small city of Marietta. And though the job I'm going to will be very interesting and challenging, and though we'll be within a couple of hours of both my wife's parents and mine, we're still leaving this area of north Georgia with a lot of mixed emotions.

For as you're all aware, these beautiful counties of Union and Towns kind of grow on you after awhile. When you combine the unbeatable scenery and the wonderful people, you have a combination that's hard to beat. If there is any place that compares to the beauty of my native West Virginia mountains and the Monongahela National Forest, it would have to be the Chattahoochee National Forest of north Georgia. We have lived in six different states, and though each one was very nice in its own way, we'd have to rank the Blairsville area at the top of our list.

It's also been a pleasure to work with all of the fine Forest Service people here. Jack McCormick is a great District Ranger and he has a top notch crew of personnel on the Brasstown Ranger District.

When our family pulled into town two short years ago, we had no idea that we would only be here for 24 months. Nor did we know we'd fall in love with this area. You all certainly do live in a "special" place. I urge all of you to show your continued interest and stay active in Forest Service programs. By doing so, you can help ensure a bright tomorrow.

I'm familiar with the Wayne National Forest, having worked there for two years back earlier in the 1970's. So, it's not like we're going somewhere that we don't know anything about. Marietta is separated from West Virginia by two bridges spanning the Ohio River. It has a lot of history, having been the first permanent settlement in the Northwest Territory, which includes the present day states of Ohio, Indiana, Illinois, Michigan, Wisconsin, and part of Minnesota.

The Marietta area is located in the foothills of the Appalachian Mountains. There are rolling hills, mostly hardwood trees with lots of Fall color, several covered bridges, a good deer and grouse population, and many fine people. Although it is difficult to leave north Georgia, the lure of getting back close to home was just too great to pass up. The opportunity might not ever come around again.

This weekly column will continue, at least in the short run, being written by Debbie Day and Frances Mason. They have filled in for me on previous occasions, so you've read their articles before. After that, perhaps my replacement will be able to continue it, if time allows. I've enjoyed writing this column and I sincerely appreciate the nice comments I have received from many of you.

I hope in some small way I've helped you to better understand and enjoy "Your .... Chattahoochee National Forest."

So long, my friends!

Here's one additional writing that I did while working in Blairsville. The local phone company approached us about using a photo of Brasstown Bald Visitor Center for its cover in 1980. (I'm pretty sure it was for 1980. That was over 30 years ago and my memory isn't what it once was.) In addition, the phone company requested that we write a short piece for the back cover, which would talk about the photo on the front cover. Since I was writing a weekly outdoor column for the local newspaper at that time, it was suggested that I do the write-up for the back cover. I was happy and honored to do so.

For the previous couple of years the phone company had featured: 1) a write-up by John Kollock, the noted historian, artist, and author from north Georgia. His write-up was a short history of northeast Georgia, along with a front cover featuring many of his scenes and depictions of those times; and, 2) a write-up by John Earl telling about the famous naturalist John Muir's walk through Georgia in 1867. Muir had hiked near Blairsville and marveled at the scenery and the hospitality of the local mountain people. The front cover was a photograph of one of north Georgia's beautiful waterfalls.

So, for the phone company to feature the Chattahoochee National Forest and Brasstown Bald Visitor Center on its cover, and for me to do the write-up, was indeed an honor and an opportunity that we just couldn't pass up.

Here is the write-up. I hope you enjoy it.

BRASSTOWN BALD VISITOR CENTER

High atop Brasstown Bald Mountain, at an elevation of 4,784 feet above sea level, sits the U.S. Forest Service's Visitor Information Center. From this lofty perch on Georgia's highest peak, visitors can survey the panoramic beauty of the surrounding mountains and valleys. On clear days the view includes South Carolina, North Carolina, Tennessee, and even downtown Atlanta, which is nearly 100 miles away.

In addition to providing the best observational platform in the entire state,

Brasstown Bald offers visitors the chance to experience cool temperatures and fluctuating weather patterns; to study or photograph the beautiful and unique vegetation; and to see the exhibits and slide programs in the Visitor Center.

Summertime temperatures at Brasstown Bald normally range from the mid 70's in the daytime to the low 50's at night. The highest temperature ever recorded was 84 degrees, while the lowest was 27 degrees below zero. Clouds often envelop the summit even while it is clear in the valleys below. Snow has fallen during every month of the year, except July and August. This, coupled with the often strong winds, helps create perhaps the harshest environment in Georgia. Winds in excess of 80 miles per hour have been recorded and have been known to cause rain to travel horizontally across the mountain for long distances before falling to the ground.

The flora surrounding Brasstown Bald has attracted thousands of botanists and nature lovers over the years. Here one can find plants that are uncommon elsewhere, or be delighted to see northern species that are unusual in Georgia, but plentiful as far north as New England, Canada, and the Great Lakes States. On Brasstown Bald's slopes you can see trees such as beech, black cherry, mountain-ash, yellow birch, silver bell, and yellow wood; or view plants and flowers like ginseng, ramps, pink and yellow ladies slippers, and jack-in-the-pulpit. Most popular among visitors are the colorful azaleas and the beautiful purple rhododendron.

The Visitor Center itself attracts tourists from all over the world. Built in 1966, the unique structure has become one of the most widely recognized landmarks in the Southeast. Visitors have come from every state in the Union and from over 50 foreign countries.

Displayed at the Visitor Center are exhibits whose theme is "Man and the Mountain;" these exhibits trace the human and natural history of the entire southern Appalachian region. A particular favorite is the talking model of a Forest Ranger, who relates his experiences on the Chattahoochee National Forest during the 1920's and 1930's. Also very popular is the "Four Seasons" slide program depicting the extreme weather changes that occur at Brasstown Bald each year. The Center is open daily from Memorial Day through the Fall color season from 9:30 a.m. to 6:00 p.m. During these hours, information specialists are available to interpret the exhibits and to answer visitors' questions.

Visit Brasstown Bald Visitor Center – a unique building, surrounded by unusual vegetation, and located midst the unequaled beauty of the North Georgia mountains!